FOR ORGANS, PIANOS & ELECTRONIC KEYBOARDS

E-Z PLAY® TODAY

27

60 Of The World's Easiest To Play Songs With 3 Chords

T0048377

ISBN 0-7935-4424-6

HAL•LEONARD®
CORPORATION

7777 W. BLUEMOUND RD. P.O. BOX 13819 MILWAUKEE, WI 53213

ALOHA OE
(Farewell To Thee)

Registration 7
Rhythm: Fox Trot or Swing

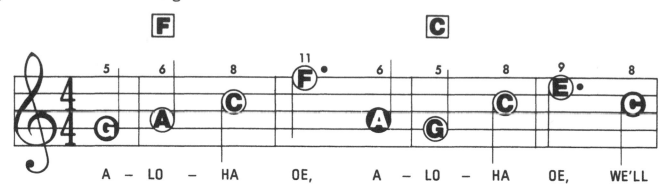

A - LO - HA OE, A - LO - HA OE, WE'LL

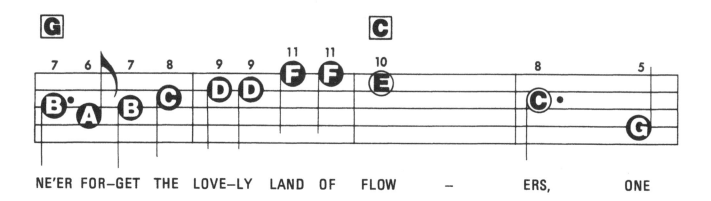

NE'ER FOR-GET THE LOVE-LY LAND OF FLOW — ERS, ONE

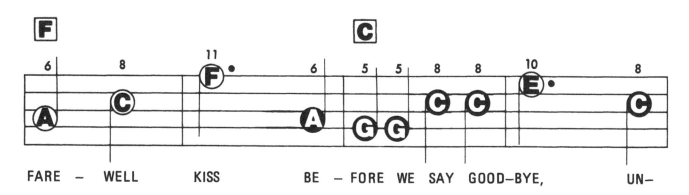

FARE — WELL KISS BE - FORE WE SAY GOOD-BYE, UN-

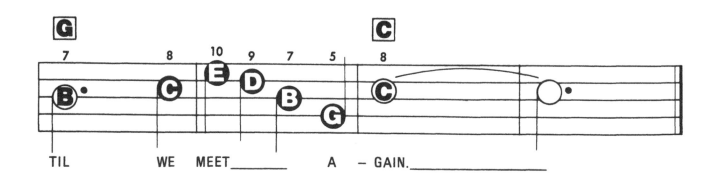

TIL WE MEET_____ A - GAIN._____

AMAZING GRACE

Registration 1
Rhythm: Waltz

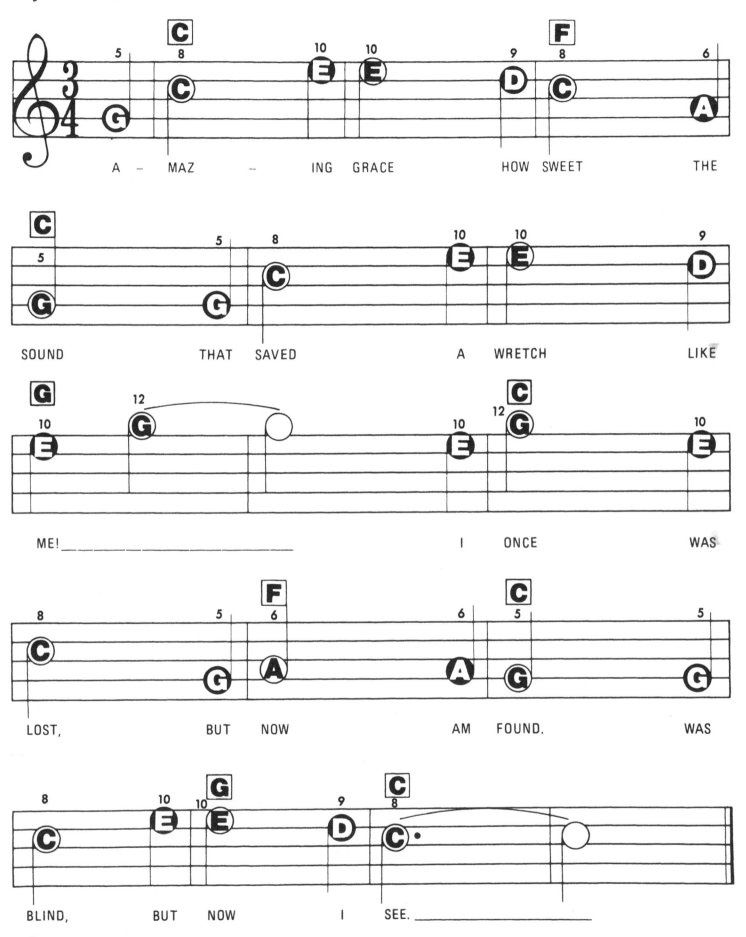

ANNIE LAURIE

Registration 3
Rhythm: Fox Trot or Swing

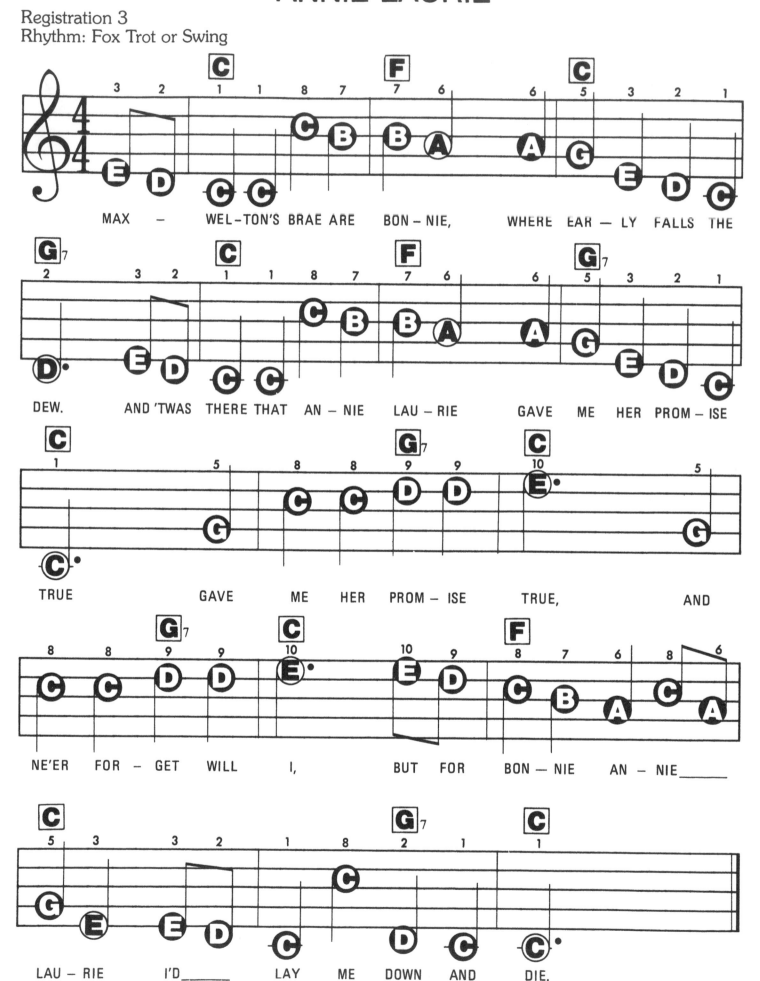

BARCAROLLE

Registration 10
Rhythm: Fox Trot or Swing

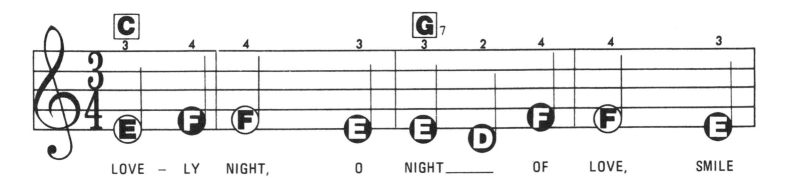

LOVE – LY NIGHT, O NIGHT____ OF LOVE, SMILE

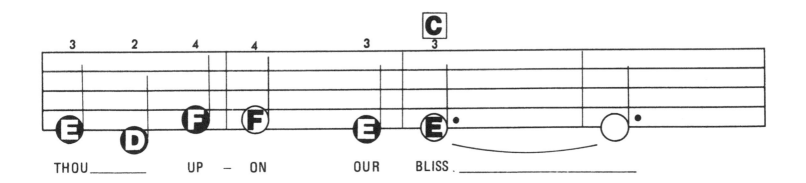

THOU____ UP – ON OUR BLISS. _____

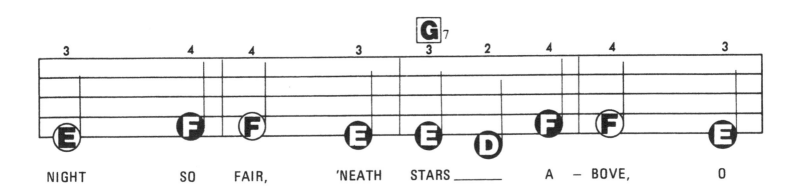

NIGHT SO FAIR, 'NEATH STARS____ A – BOVE, O

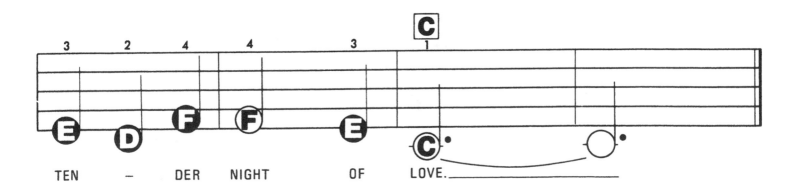

TEN – DER NIGHT OF LOVE. _____

ARKANSAS TRAVELER

Registration 8
Rhythm: Waltz

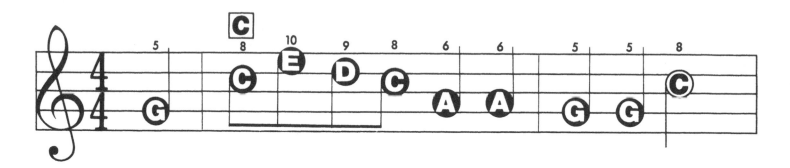

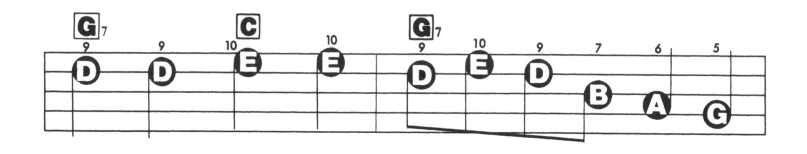

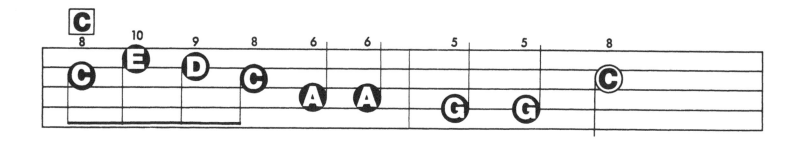

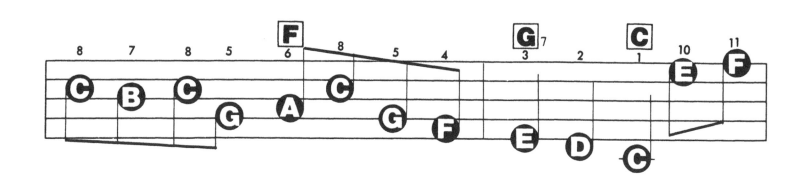

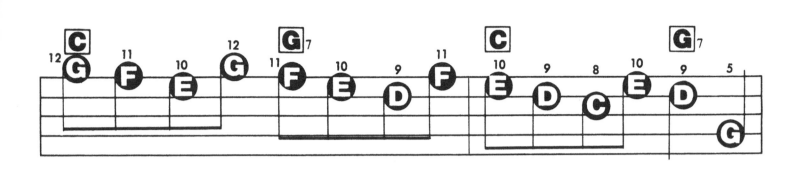

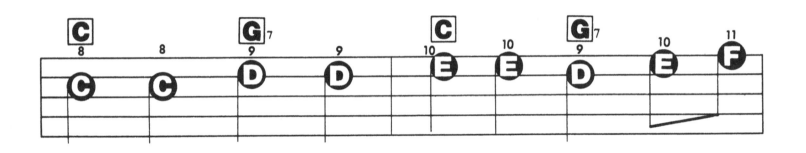

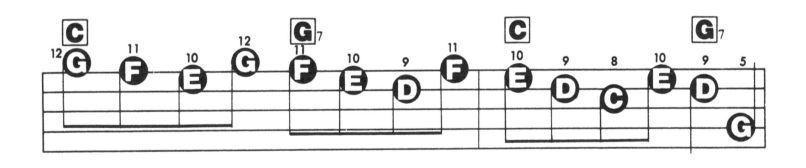

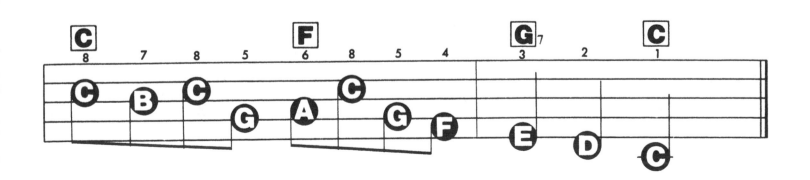

BEAUTIFUL DREAMER

Registration 9
Rhythm: Waltz

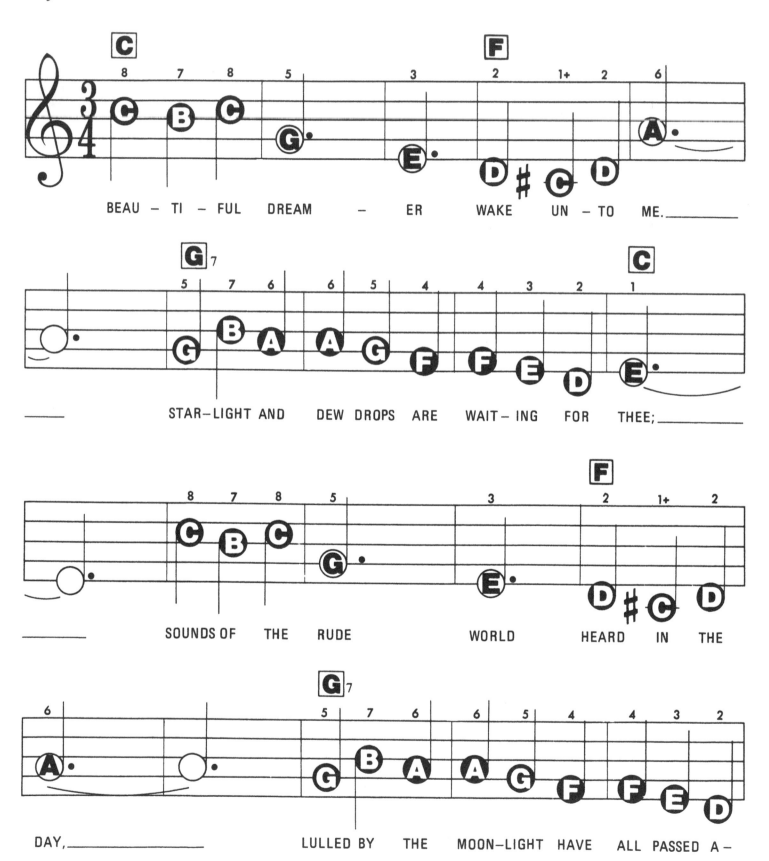

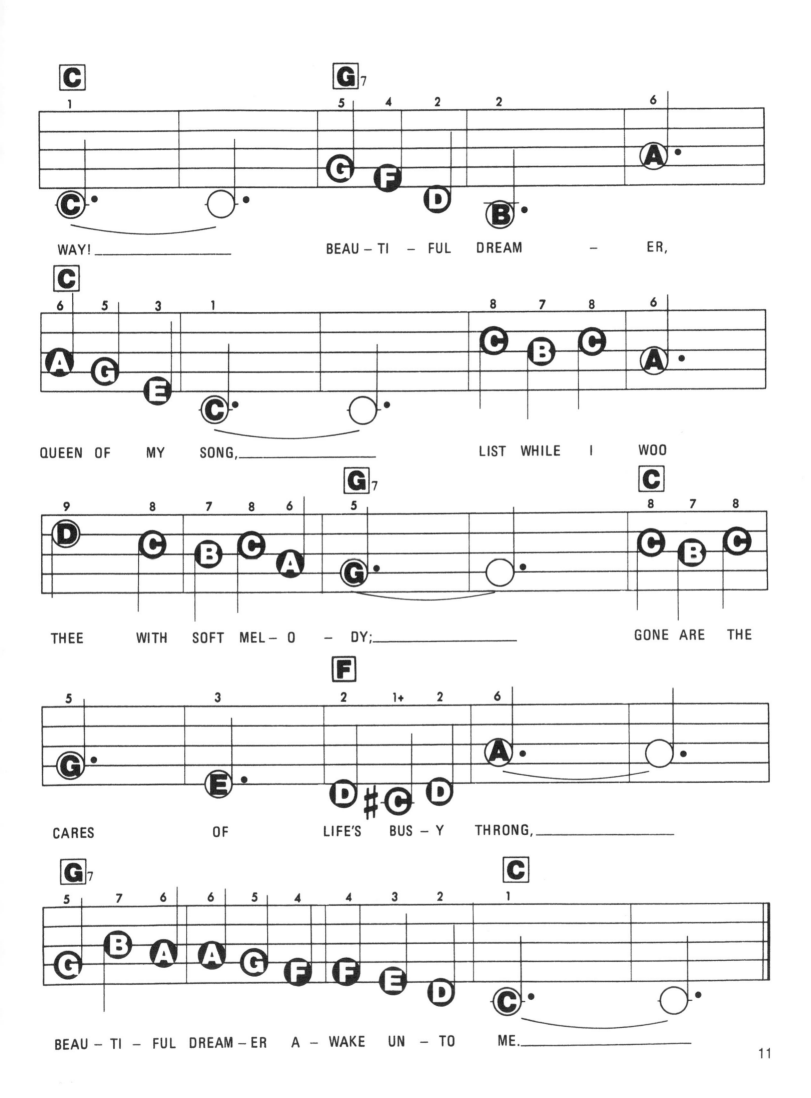

WAY! _____ BEAU – TI – FUL DREAM – ER,

QUEEN OF MY SONG,_____ LIST WHILE I WOO

THEE WITH SOFT MEL – O – DY;_____ GONE ARE THE

CARES OF LIFE'S BUS – Y THRONG,_____

BEAU – TI – FUL DREAM – ER A – WAKE UN – TO ME._____

BEDELIA

Registration 4
Rhythm: Fox Trot or Swing

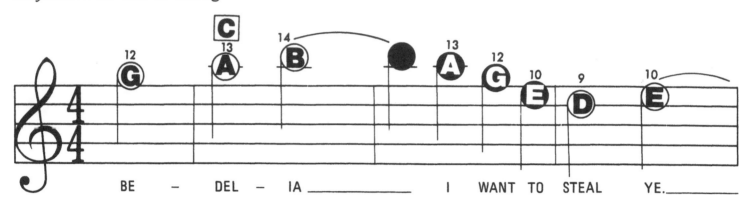

BE — DEL — IA _____ I WANT TO STEAL YE.

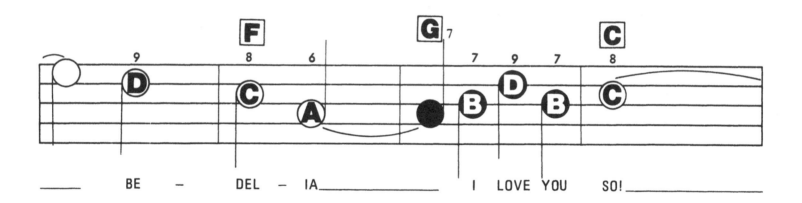

_____ BE — DEL — IA_____ I LOVE YOU SO! _____

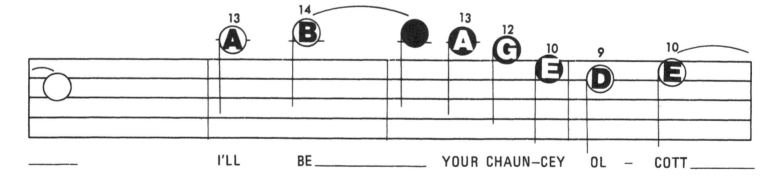

_____ I'LL BE_____ YOUR CHAUN—CEY OL — COTT_____

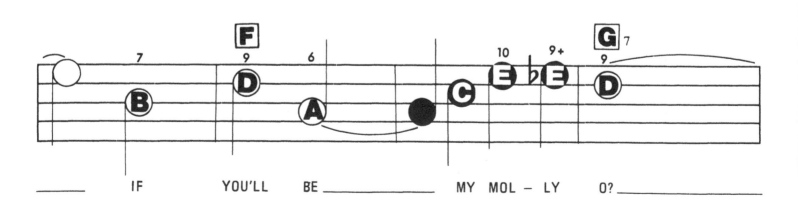

_____ IF YOU'LL BE_____ MY MOL — LY O?_____

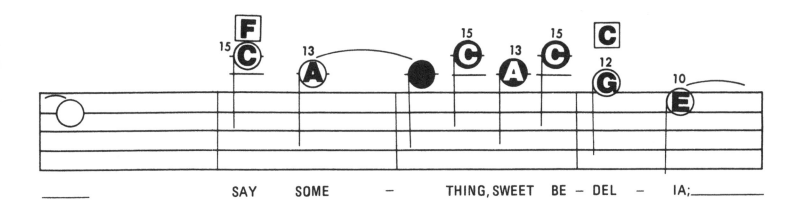

SAY SOME – THING, SWEET BE – DEL – IA; _____

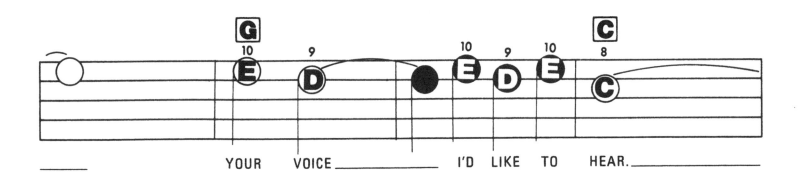

YOUR VOICE _____ I'D LIKE TO HEAR. _____

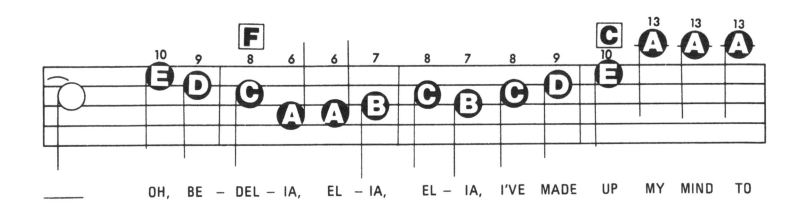

OH, BE – DEL – IA, EL – IA, EL – IA, I'VE MADE UP MY MIND TO

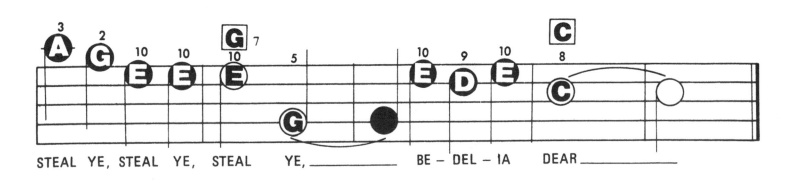

STEAL YE, STEAL YE, STEAL YE, _____ BE – DEL – IA DEAR _____

THE BIRTHDAY SONG

Registration 8
Rhythm: Waltz

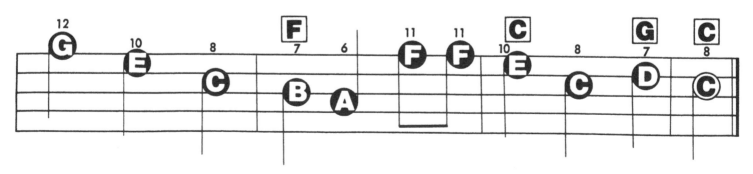

BLOW THE MAN DOWN

Registration 1
Rhythm: Waltz

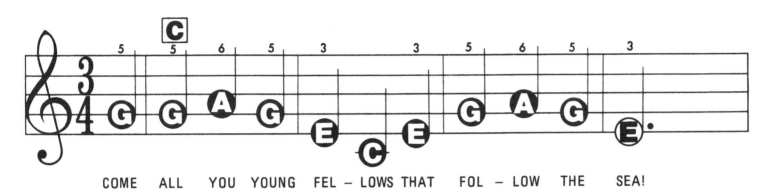

COME ALL YOU YOUNG FEL – LOWS THAT FOL – LOW THE SEA!

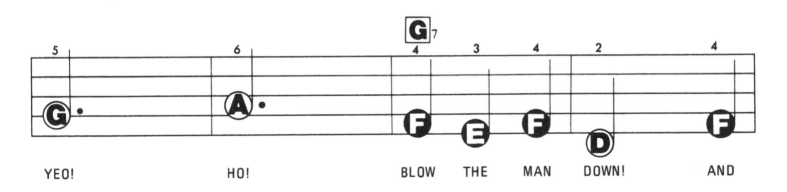

YEO! HO! BLOW THE MAN DOWN! AND

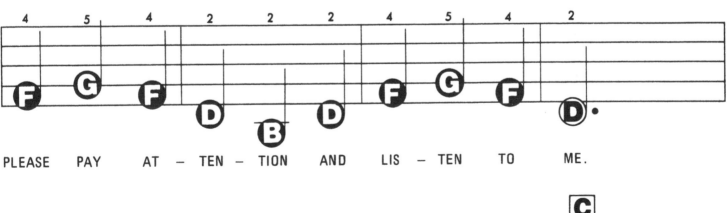

PLEASE PAY AT – TEN – TION AND LIS – TEN TO ME.

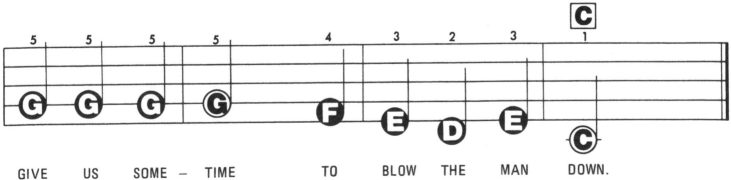

GIVE US SOME – TIME TO BLOW THE MAN DOWN.

BLUE DANUBE

Registration 10
Rhythm: Waltz

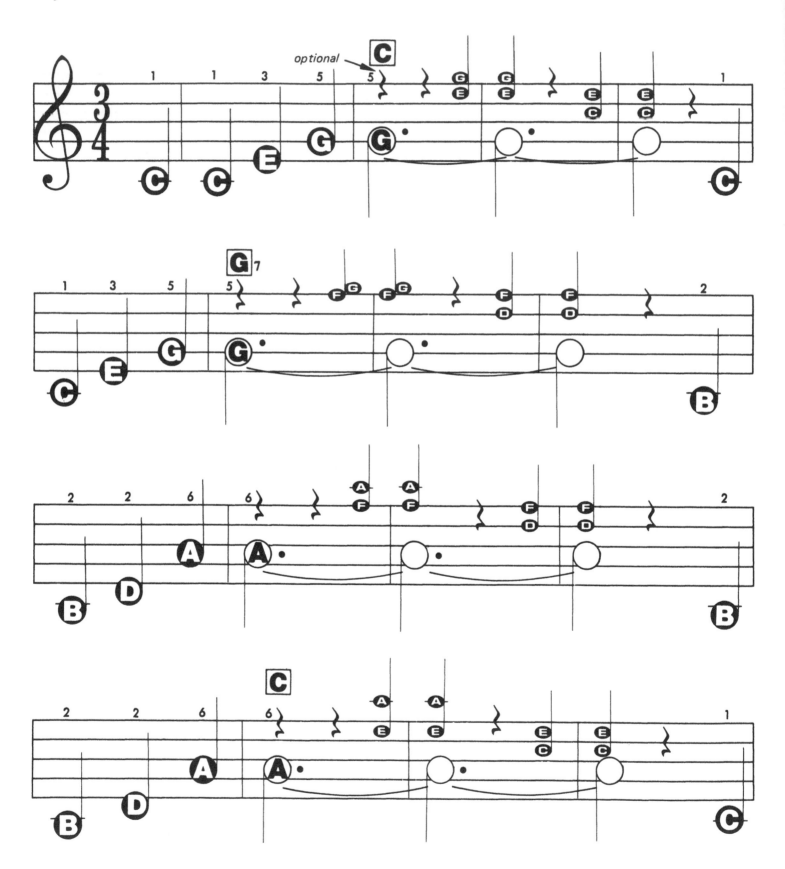

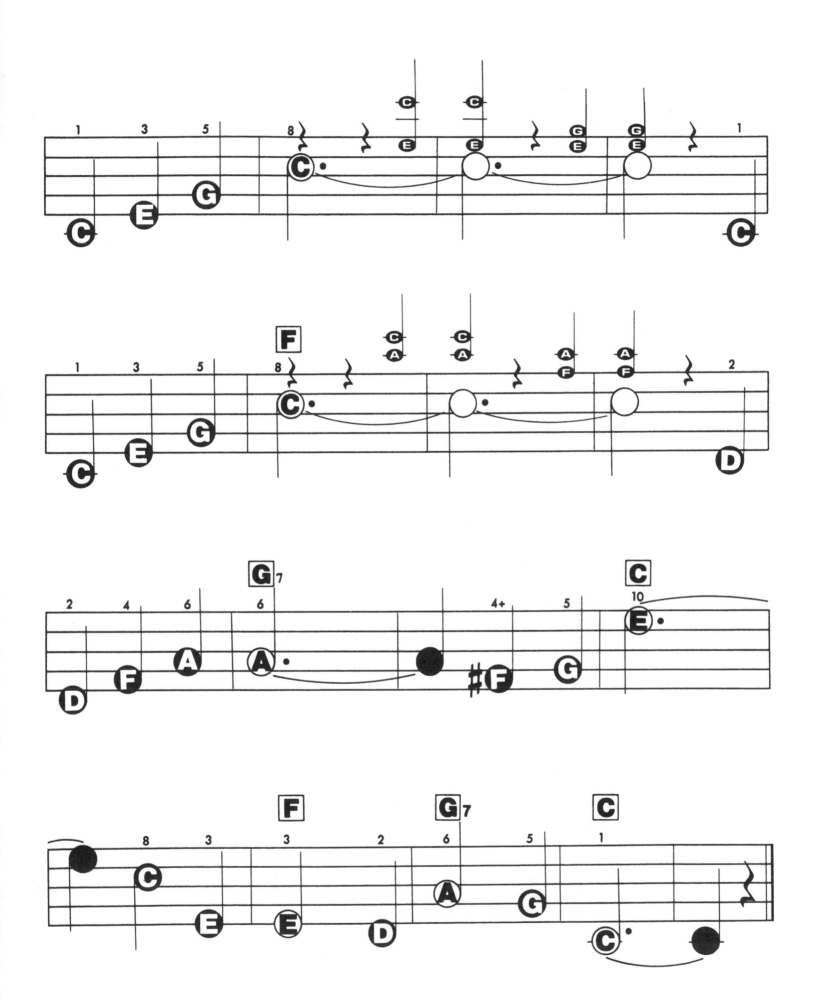

THE BOWERY

Registration 4
Rhythm: Waltz

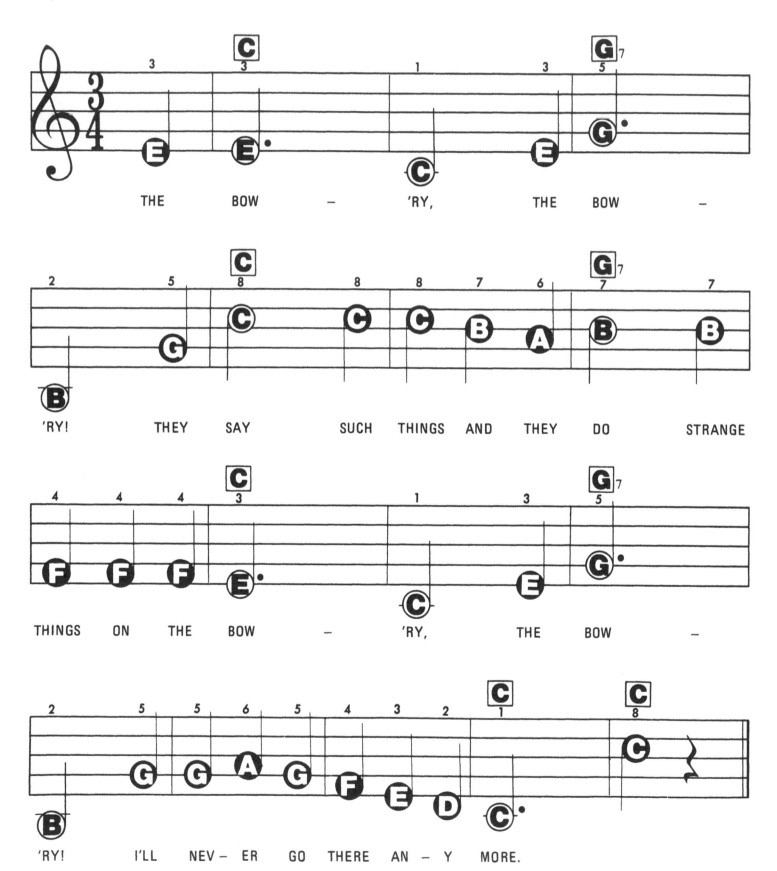

BRIDAL CHORUS

Registration 9
Rhythm: March

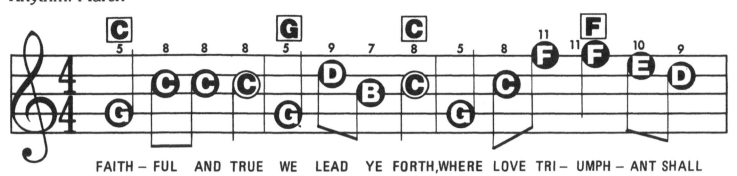

FAITH – FUL   AND   TRUE   WE   LEAD   YE   FORTH,   WHERE   LOVE   TRI – UMPH – ANT   SHALL

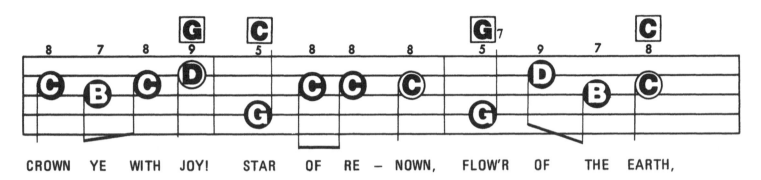

CROWN   YE   WITH   JOY!   STAR   OF   RE – NOWN,   FLOW'R   OF   THE   EARTH,

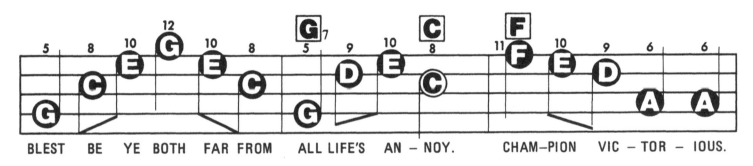

BLEST   BE   YE   BOTH   FAR   FROM   ALL   LIFE'S   AN – NOY.   CHAM–PION   VIC – TOR – IOUS.

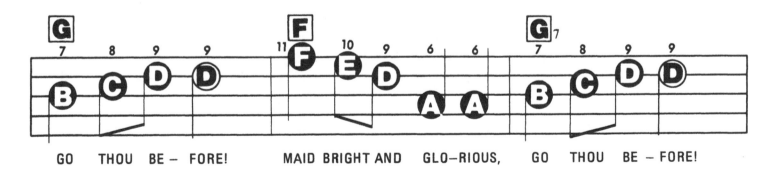

GO   THOU   BE – FORE!   MAID   BRIGHT   AND   GLO–RIOUS,   GO   THOU   BE – FORE!

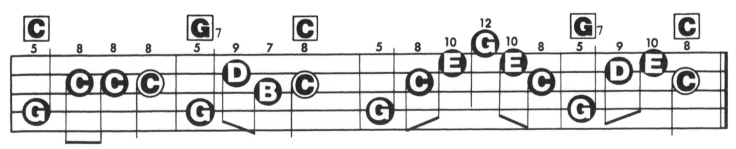

FAITH–FUL   AND   TRUE,   WE   LEAD   YE   FORTH,   WHERE LOVE TRI–UMPH–ANTSHALL CROWN YE WITH JOY!

THE CAISSONS GO ROLLING ALONG

Registration 4
Rhythm: March or Polka

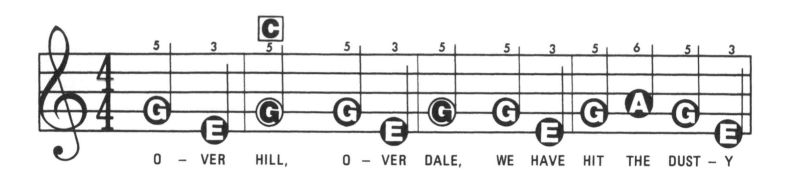

O - VER HILL, O - VER DALE, WE HAVE HIT THE DUST - Y

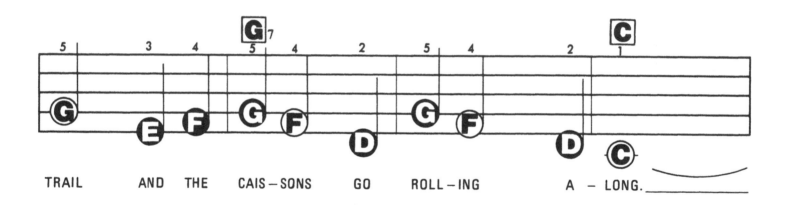

TRAIL AND THE CAIS-SONS GO ROLL-ING A - LONG.____

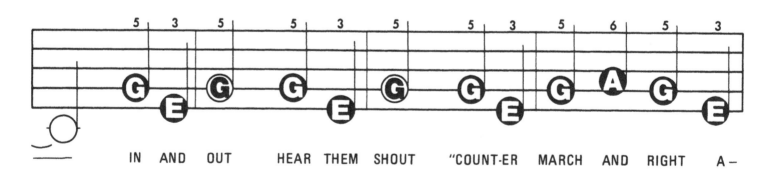

IN AND OUT HEAR THEM SHOUT "COUNT-ER MARCH AND RIGHT A-

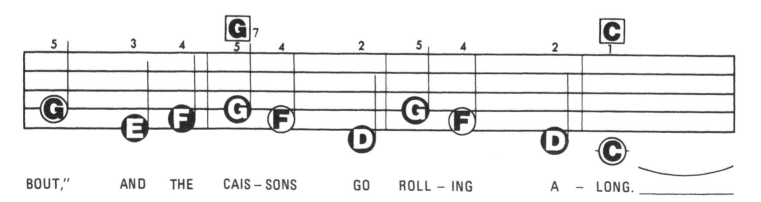

BOUT," AND THE CAIS-SONS GO ROLL-ING A - LONG.____

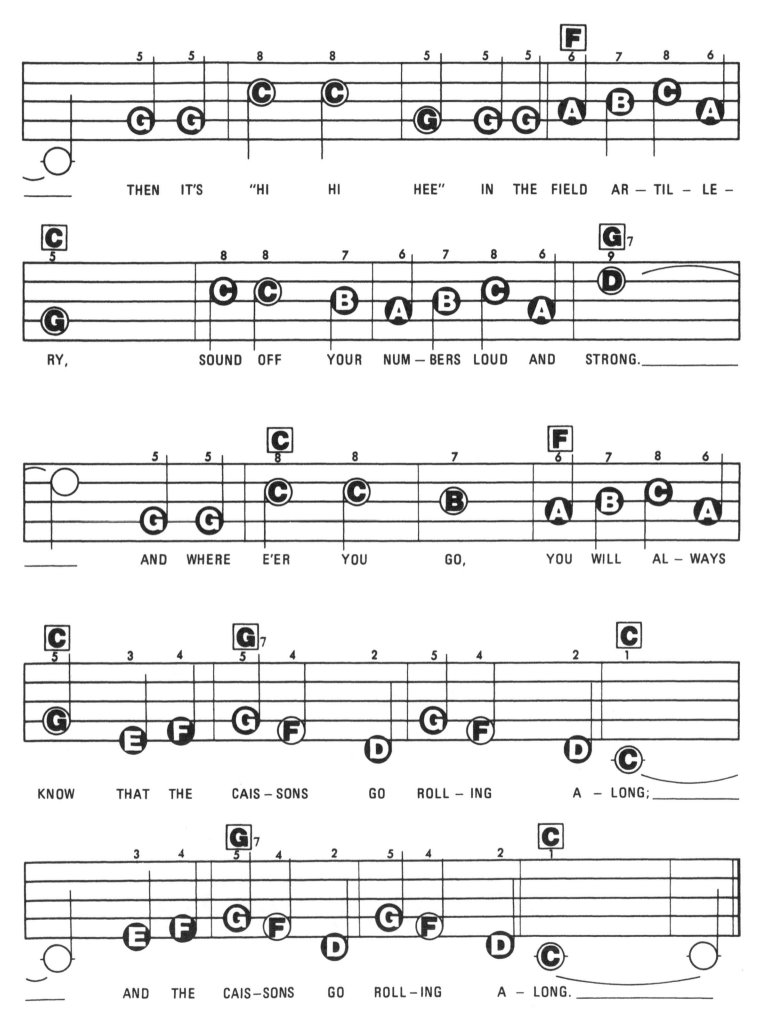

THEN IT'S "HI HI HEE" IN THE FIELD AR — TIL — LE —

RY, SOUND OFF YOUR NUM — BERS LOUD AND STRONG._____

_____ AND WHERE E'ER YOU GO, YOU WILL AL — WAYS

KNOW THAT THE CAIS — SONS GO ROLL — ING A — LONG;_____

AND THE CAIS-SONS GO ROLL-ING A — LONG._____

CAN-CAN POLKA

Registration 2
Rhythm: Polka or March

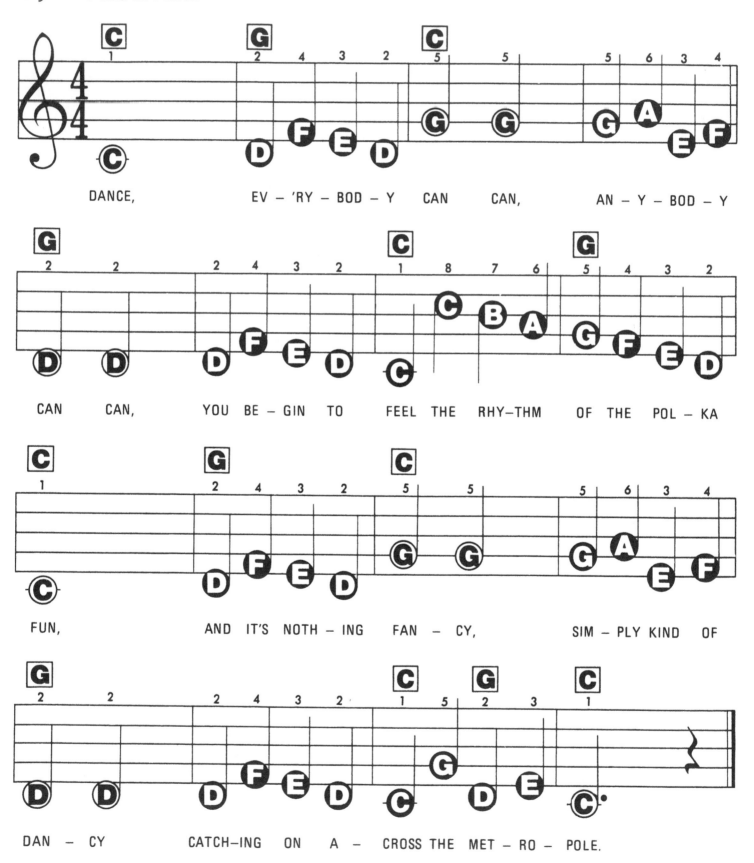

DANCE, EV – 'RY – BOD – Y CAN CAN, AN – Y – BOD – Y

CAN CAN, YOU BE – GIN TO FEEL THE RHY–THM OF THE POL – KA

FUN, AND IT'S NOTH – ING FAN – CY, SIM – PLY KIND OF

DAN – CY CATCH–ING ON A – CROSS THE MET – RO – POLE.

CARELESS LOVE

Registration 8
Rhythm: Fox Trot or Swing

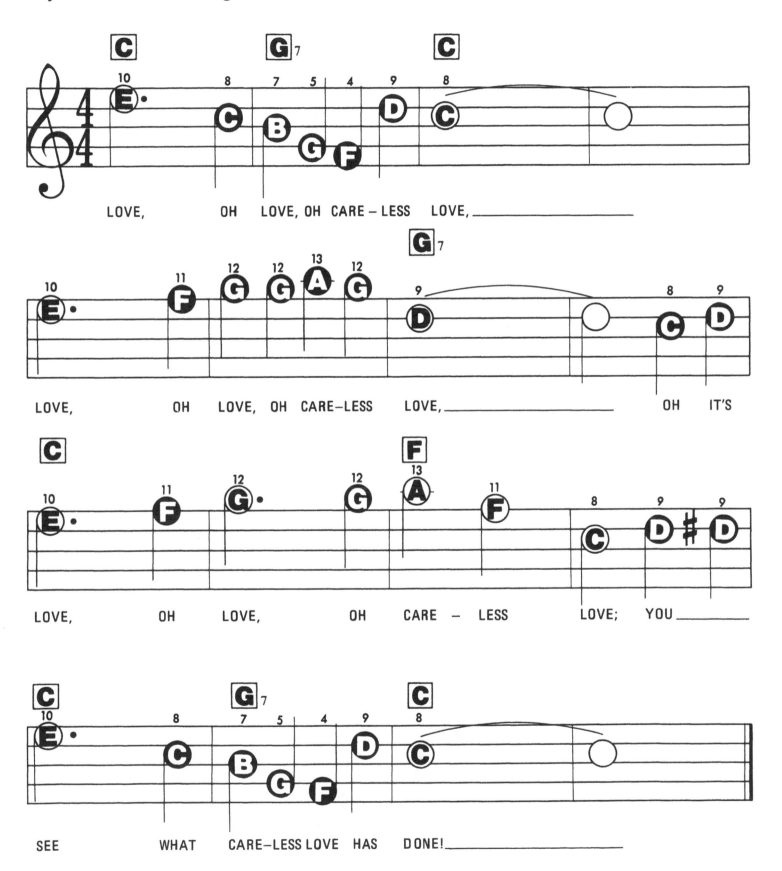

CHOPSTICKS

Registration 8
Rhythm: Waltz

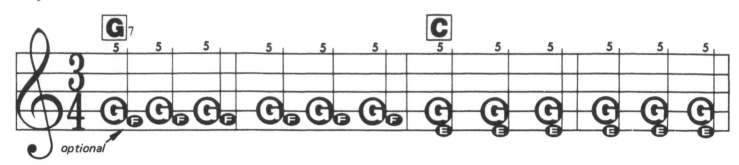

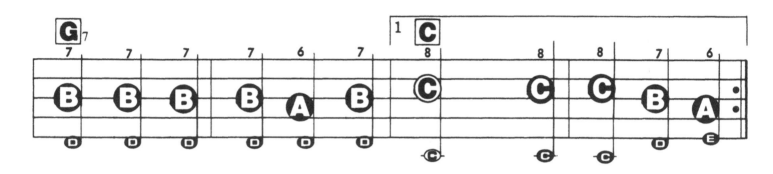

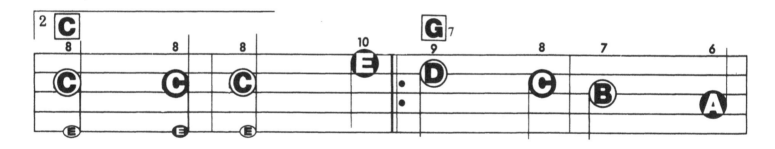

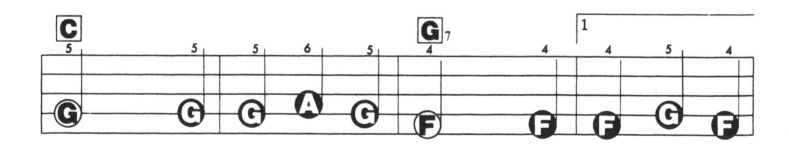

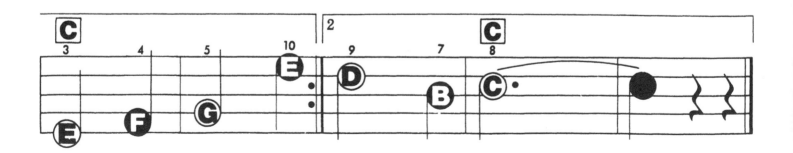

CINDY

Registration 2
Rhythm: Fox Trot or Swing

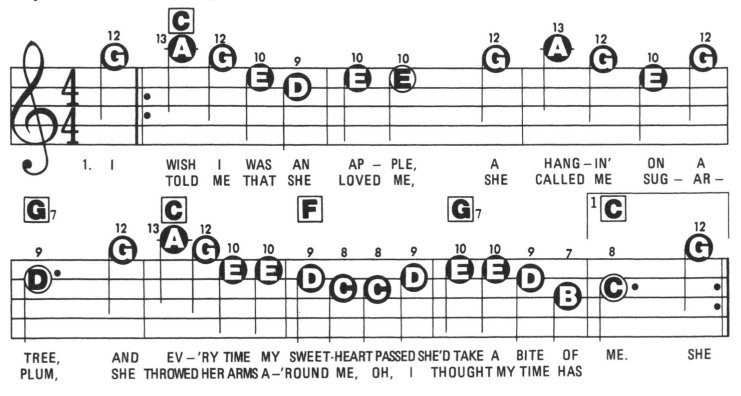

1. I WISH I WAS AN AP – PLE, A HANG – IN' ON A
   TOLD ME THAT SHE LOVED ME, SHE CALLED ME SUG – AR –

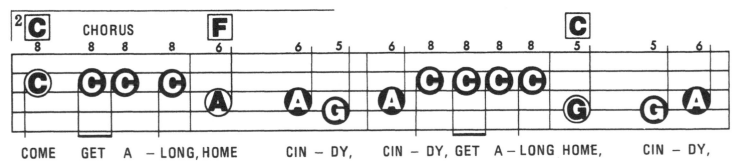

TREE, AND EV – 'RY TIME MY SWEET-HEART PASSED SHE'D TAKE A BITE OF ME. SHE
PLUM, SHE THROWED HER ARMS A – 'ROUND ME, OH, I THOUGHT MY TIME HAS

CHORUS

COME GET A – LONG, HOME CIN – DY, CIN – DY, GET A – LONG HOME, CIN – DY,

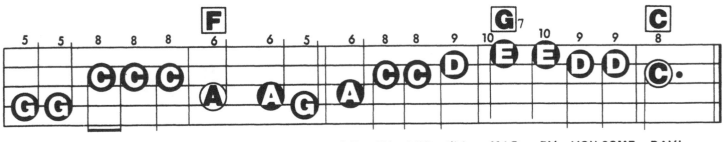

CIN – DY, GET A – LONG HOME, CIN – DY, CIN –DY AND I'LL MAR – RY YOU SOME DAY!

2. SHE TOOK ME TO THE PARLOR,
   SHE COOLED ME WITH HER FAN.
   SHE SWORE I WAS THE PURTIEST THING
   IN THE SHAPE OF MORTAL MAN.
   I WISH I HAD A NEEDLE,
   AS FINE AS I COULD SEW;
   I'D SEW THE GIRLS TO MY COAT-TAIL,
   AND DOWN THE ROAD I'D GO!
   CHORUS

3. THEN CINDY GOT RELIGION,
   SHE HAD IT ONCE BEFORE;
   BUT WHEN SHE HEARD MY OLD BANJO,
   SHE'S THE FIRST ONE ON THE FLOOR.
   SO CINDY WENT TO PREACHIN',
   SHE SWUNG AROUND AND 'ROUND;
   SHE GOT SO FULL OF GLORY
   SHE KNOCKED THE PREACHER DOWN!
   CHORUS

CIELITO LINDO

Registration 5
Rhythm: Waltz

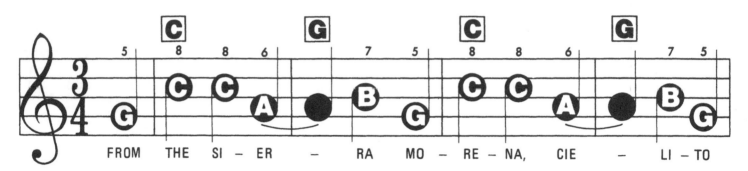

FROM THE SI — ER — RA MO — RE — NA, CIE — LI — TO

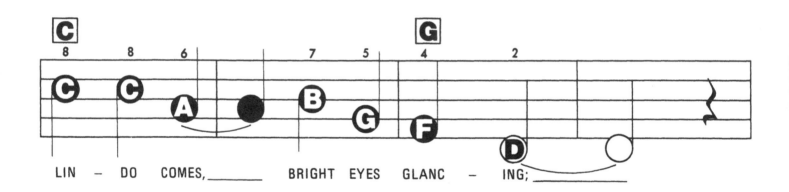

LIN — DO COMES,_____ BRIGHT EYES GLANC — ING;_____

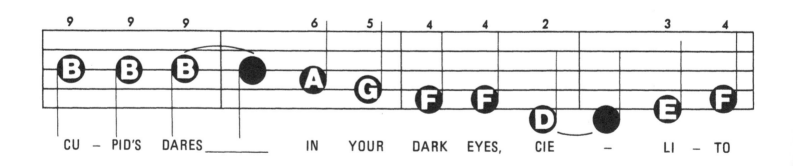

CU — PID'S DARES_____ IN YOUR DARK EYES, CIE — LI — TO

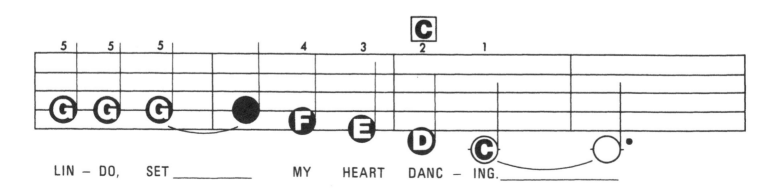

LIN — DO, SET _____ MY HEART DANC — ING._____

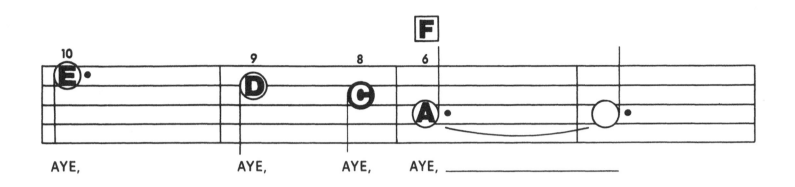

AYE,   AYE,   AYE,   AYE, _____

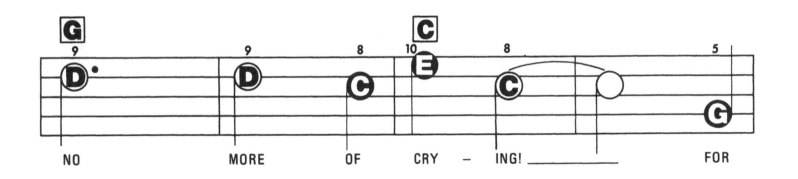

NO   MORE   OF   CRY — ING! _____   FOR

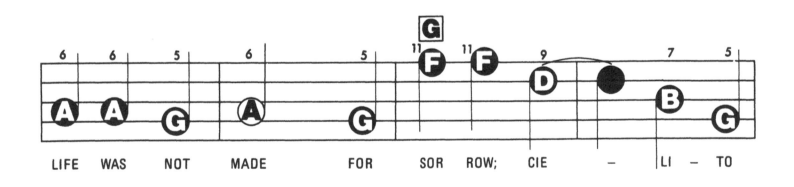

LIFE   WAS   NOT   MADE   FOR   SOR   ROW;   CIE   —   LI — TO

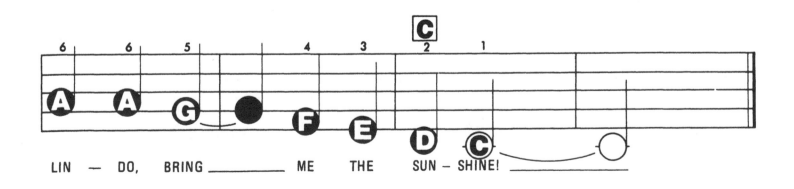

LIN — DO,   BRING _____ ME   THE   SUN — SHINE! _____

CLEMENTINE

Registration 1
Rhythm: Waltz

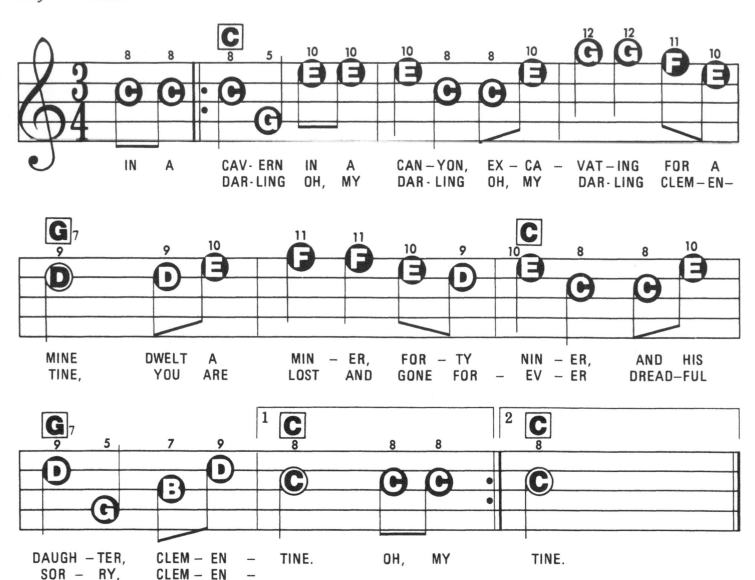

IN A CAV-ERN IN A CAN-YON, EX-CA-VAT-ING FOR A
DAR-LING OH, MY DAR-LING OH, MY DAR-LING CLEM-EN-

MINE, DWELT A MIN-ER, FOR-TY NIN-ER, AND HIS
TINE, YOU ARE LOST AND GONE FOR-EV-ER AND HIS

DAUGH-TER, CLEM-EN-TINE. OH, MY TINE.
SOR-RY, CLEM-EN-

GIT ALONG LITTLE DOGGIES

Registration 3
Rhythm: Waltz

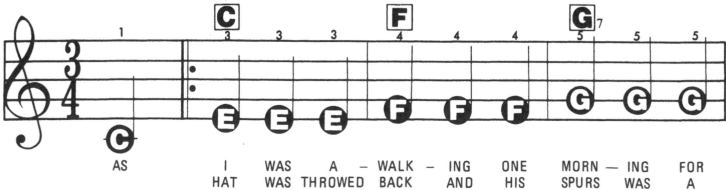

AS I WAS A-WALK-ING ONE MORN-ING FOR
HAT WAS THROWED BACK AND HIS SPURS WAS A

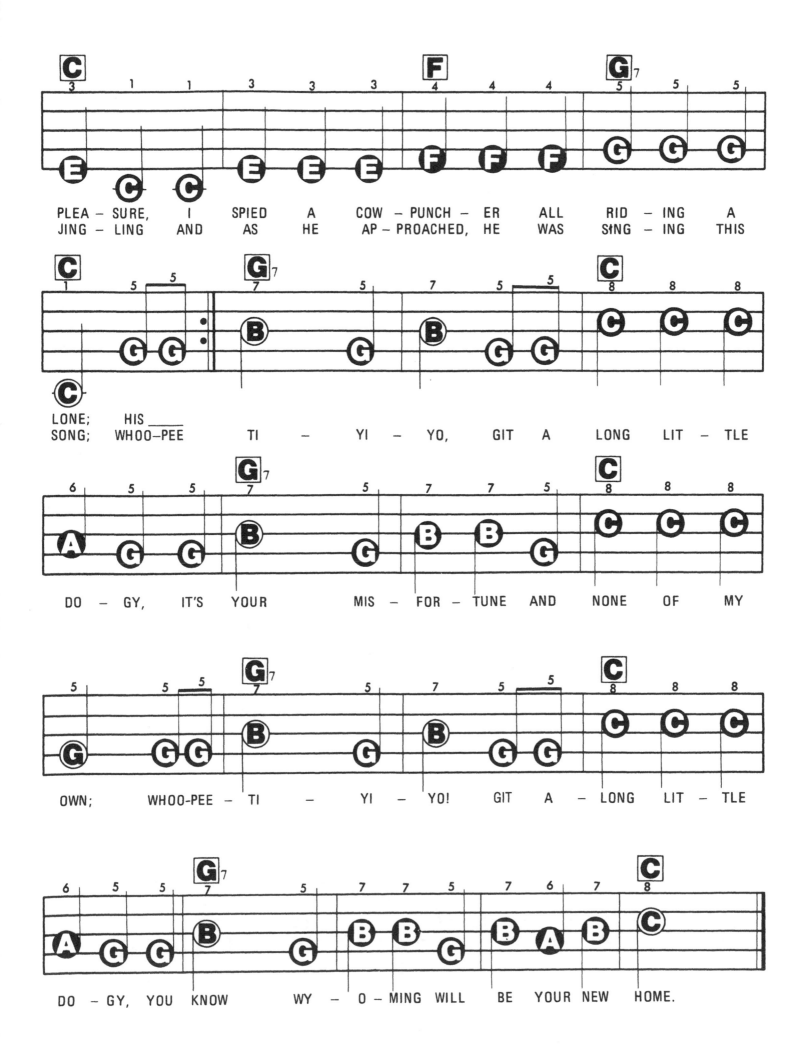

COUNTRY GARDENS

Registration 2
Rhythm: Fox Trot or Swing

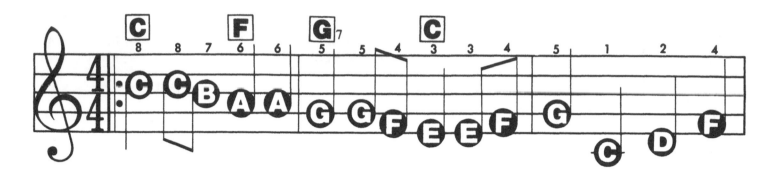

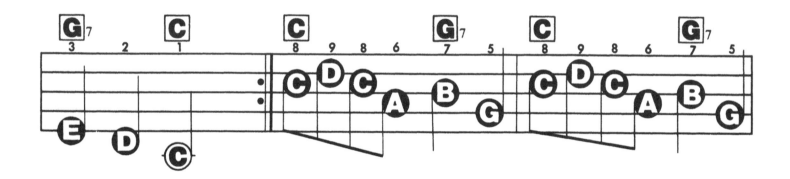

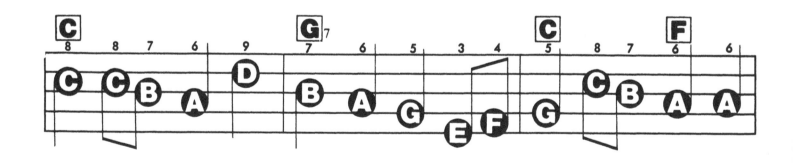

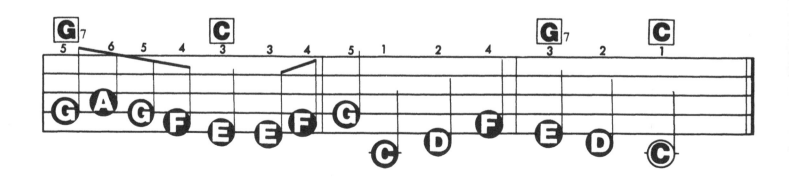

DRINK TO ME ONLY WITH THINE EYES

Registration 8
Rhythm: Waltz

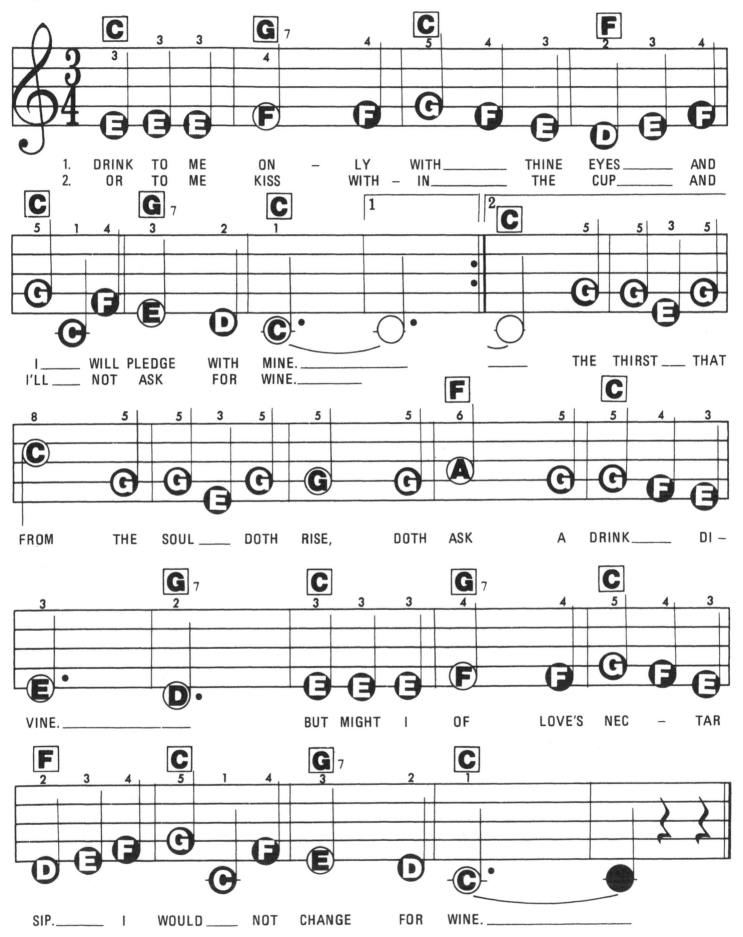

DU, DU, LIEGST MIR IM HERZEN

Registration 9
Rhythm: Waltz

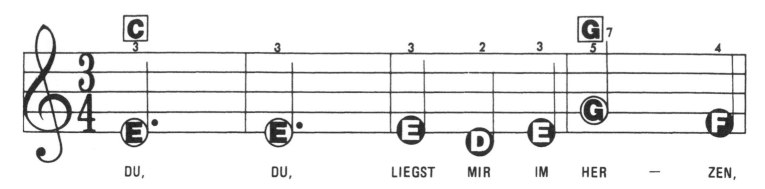

DU,   DU,   LIEGST MIR IM HER — ZEN,

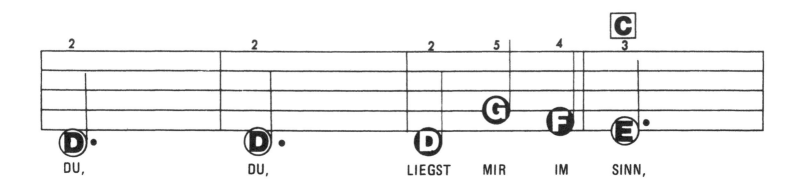

DU,   DU,   LIEGST MIR IM SINN,

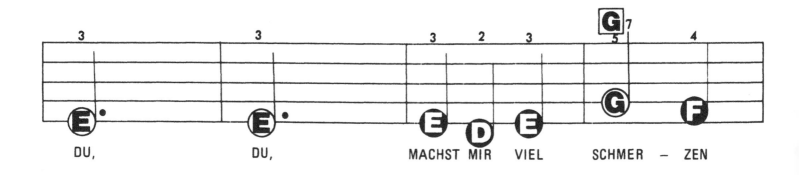

DU,   DU,   MACHST MIR VIEL SCHMER — ZEN

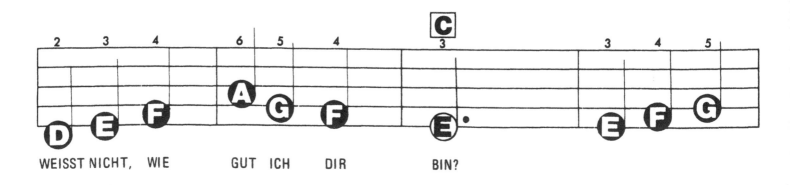

WEISST NICHT, WIE   GUT ICH DIR   BIN?

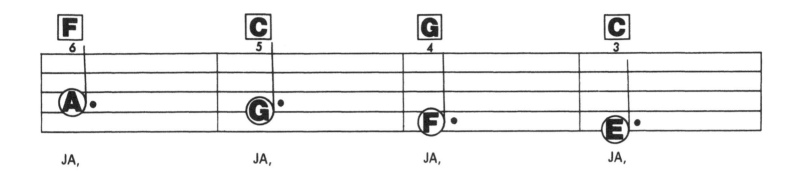

JA,   JA,   JA,   JA,

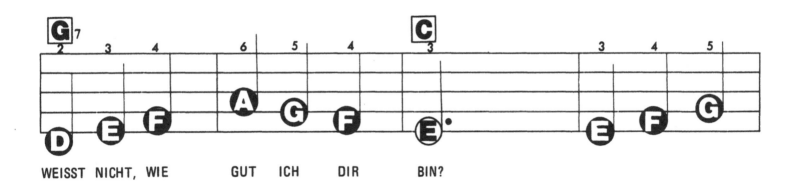

WEISST NICHT, WIE   GUT ICH DIR BIN?

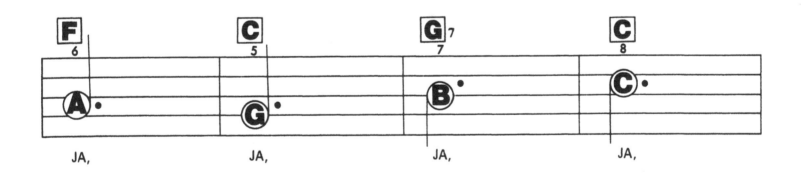

JA,   JA,   JA,   JA,

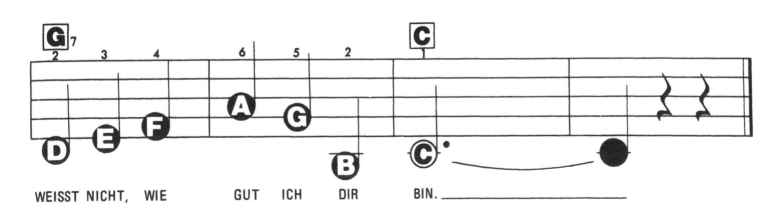

WEISST NICHT, WIE   GUT ICH DIR BIN. _____

ESPANA

Registration 9
Rhythm: Waltz

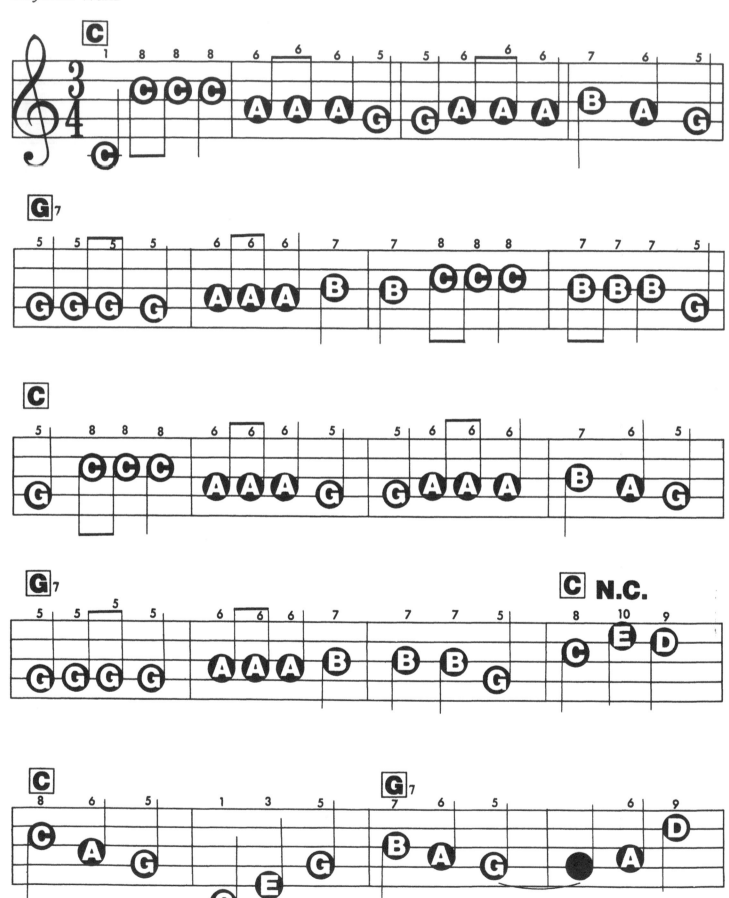

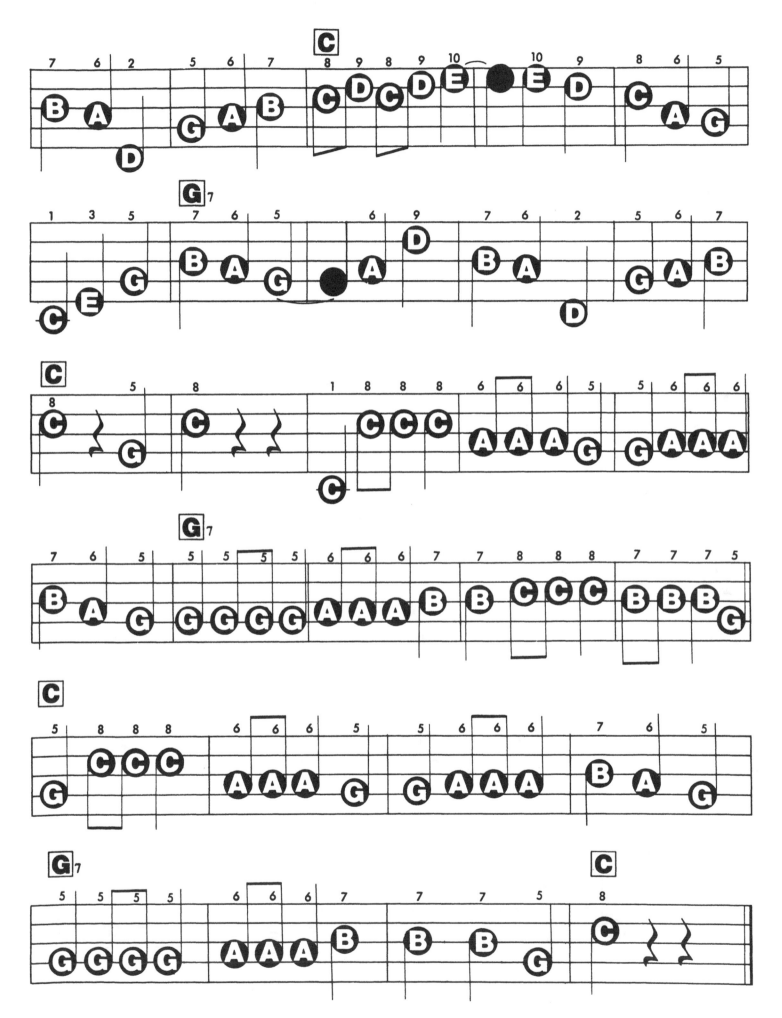

FOR HE'S A JOLLY GOOD FELLOW

Registration 2
Rhythm: Waltz

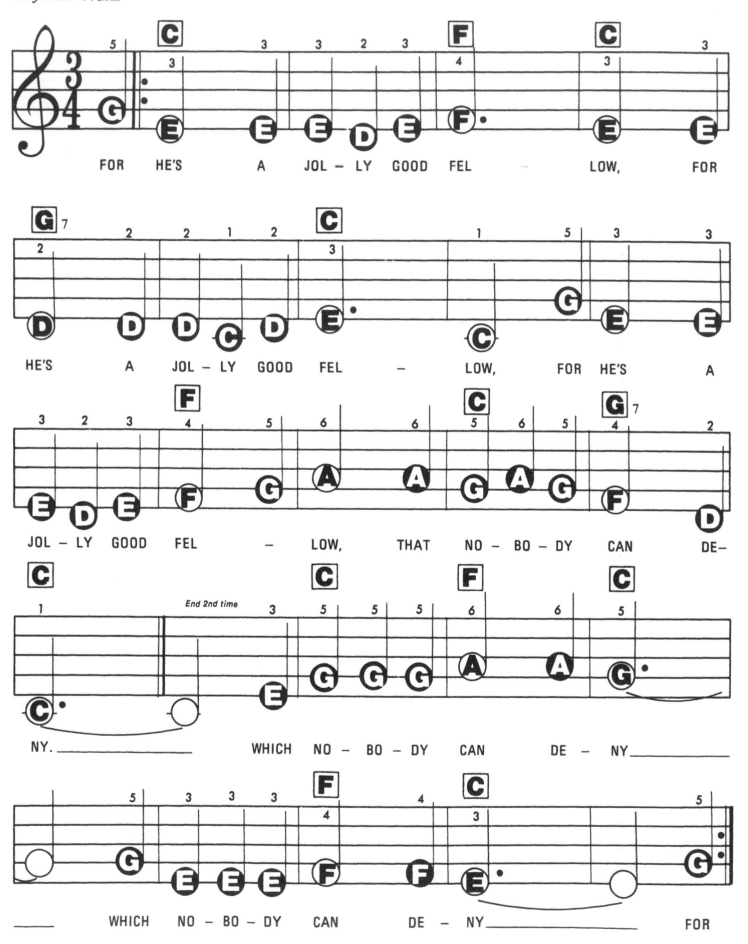

HUMORESKE

Registration 8
Rhythm: Fox Trot or Swing

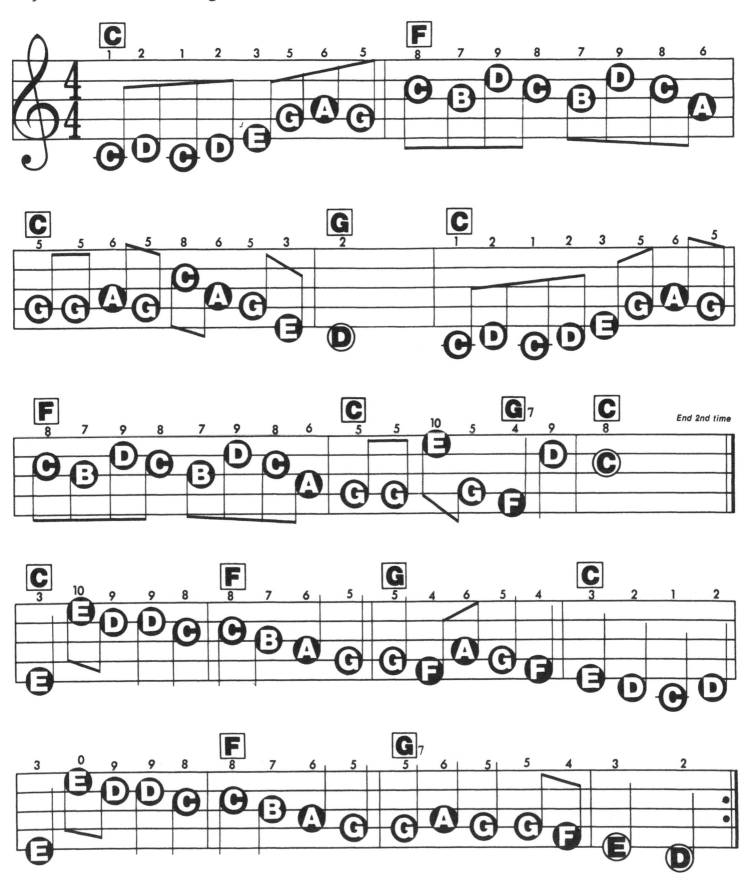

FRANKIE AND JOHNNY

Registration 7
Rhythm: Swing

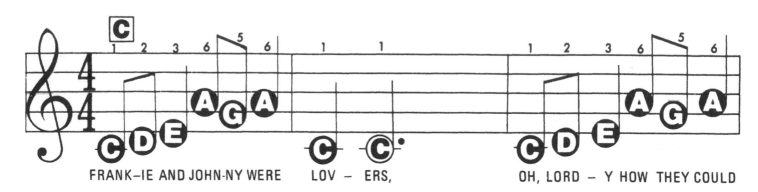

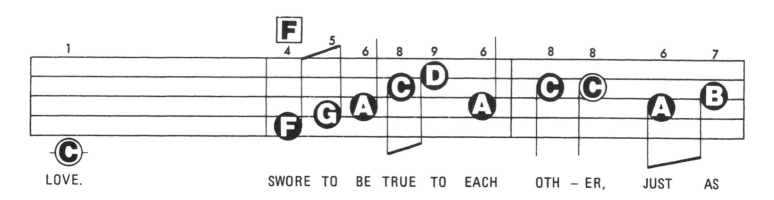

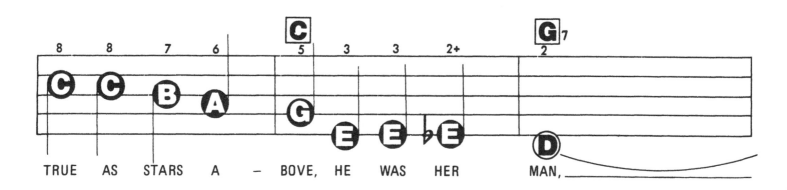

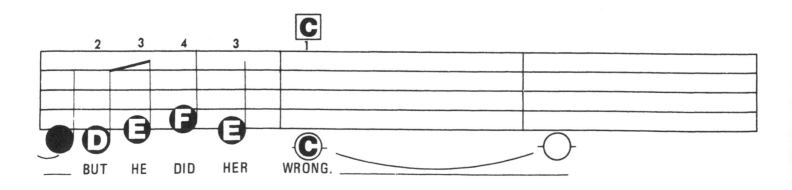

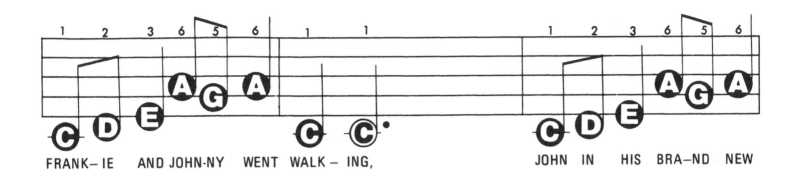

FRANK—IE AND JOHN-NY WENT WALK—ING, JOHN IN HIS BRA—ND NEW

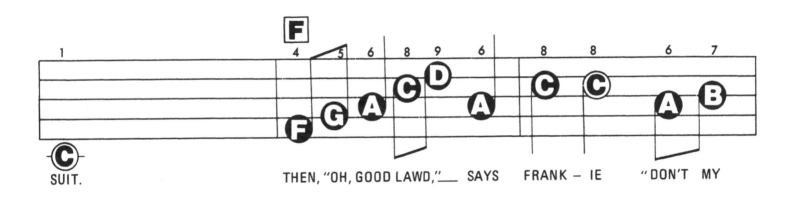

SUIT. THEN, "OH, GOOD LAWD,"___ SAYS FRANK — IE "DON'T MY

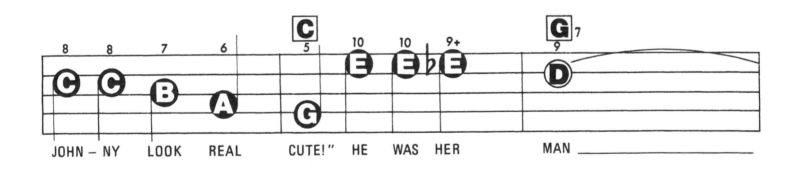

JOHN — NY LOOK REAL CUTE!" HE WAS HER MAN ___

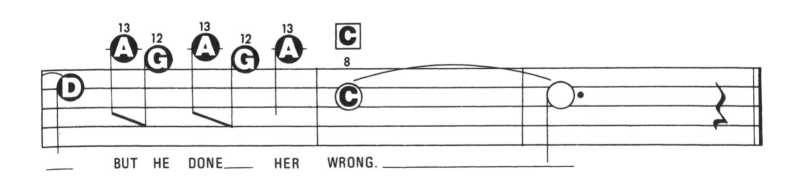

___ BUT HE DONE___ HER WRONG. ___

HOME, SWEET HOME

Registration 1
Rhythm: Waltz

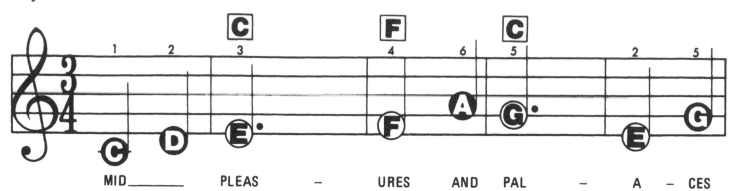

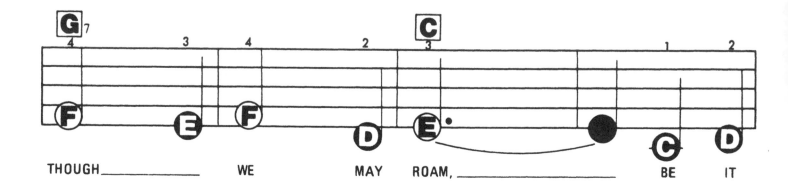

MID____ PLEAS – URES AND PAL – A – CES

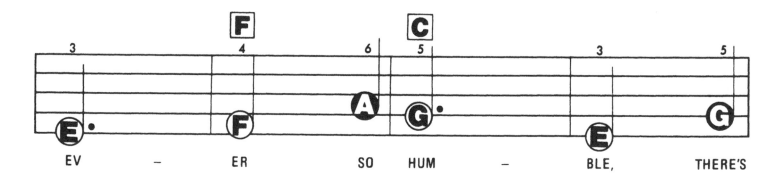

THOUGH_____ WE MAY ROAM,_____ BE IT

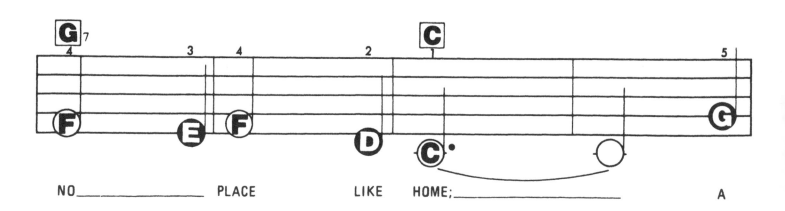

EV – ER SO HUM – BLE, THERE'S

NO_____ PLACE LIKE HOME;_____ A

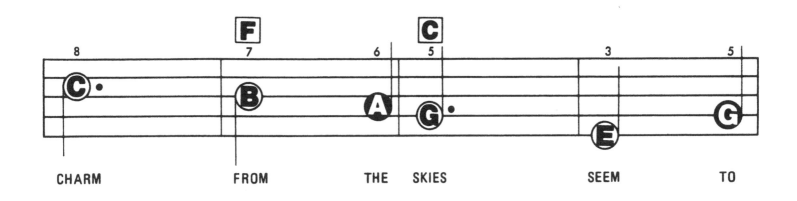

CHARM   FROM   THE   SKIES   SEEM   TO

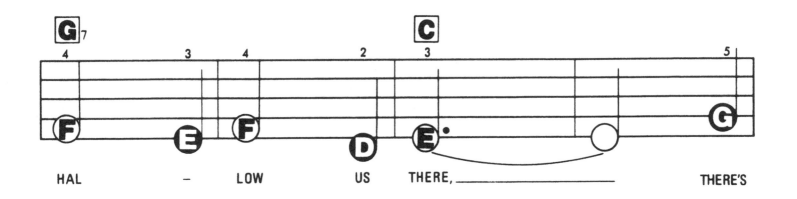

HAL   -   LOW   US   THERE,_____ THERE'S

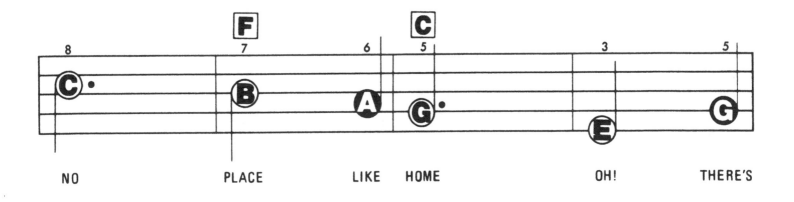

NO   PLACE   LIKE   HOME   OH!   THERE'S

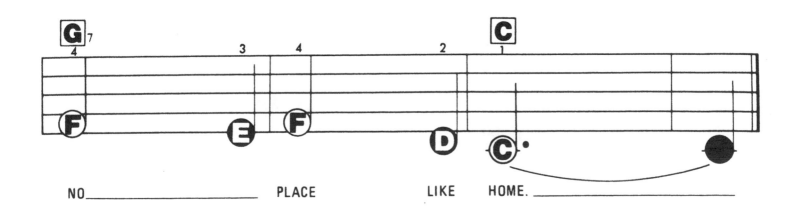

NO_____ PLACE   LIKE   HOME._____

IMMER NOCH EIN TROEPFCHEN

(O, Susanna Schottische)

Registration 2
Rhythm: Fox Trot or Swing

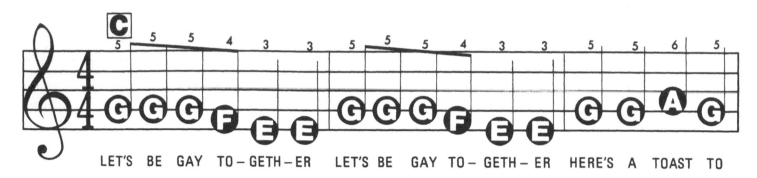

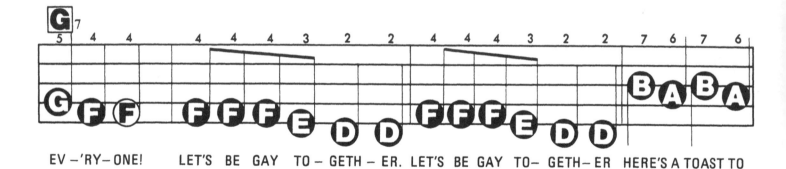

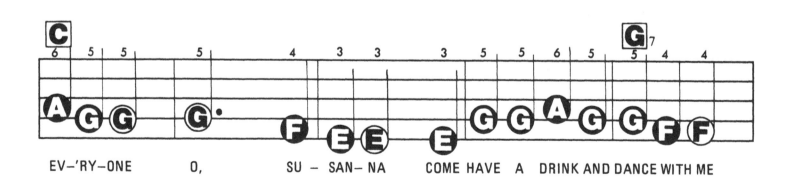

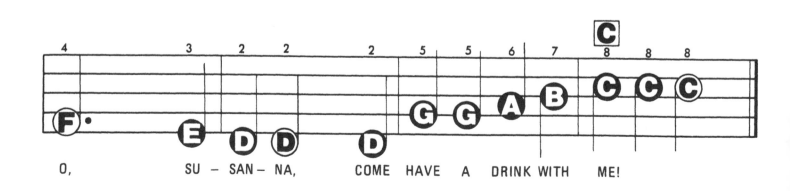

IN THE EVENING BY THE MOONLIGHT

Registration 4
Rhythm: Fox Trot or Swing

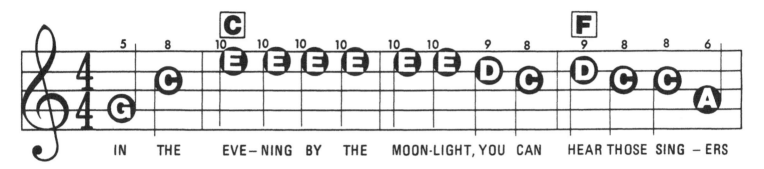

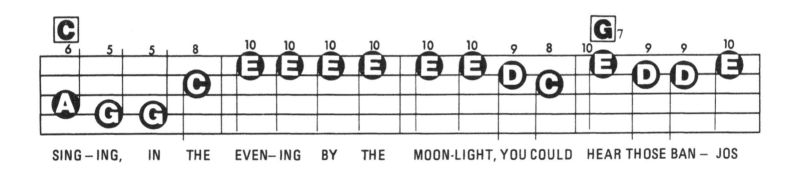

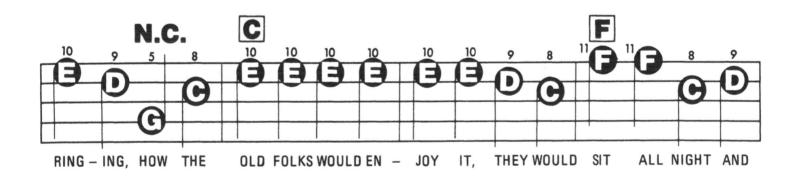

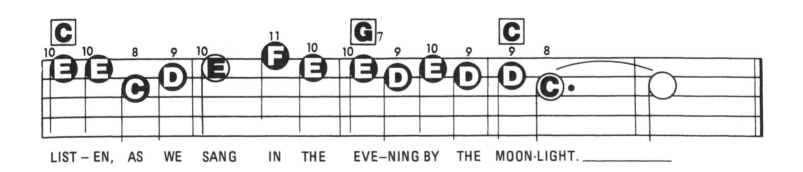

GRANDFATHER'S CLOCK

Registration 4
Rhythm: Fox Trot or Swing

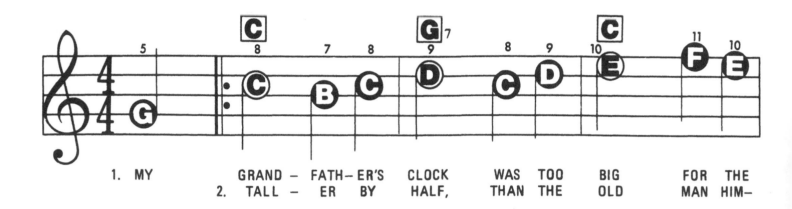

1. MY GRAND — FATH—ER'S CLOCK WAS TOO BIG FOR THE
2. TALL — ER BY HALF, THAN THE OLD MAN HIM—

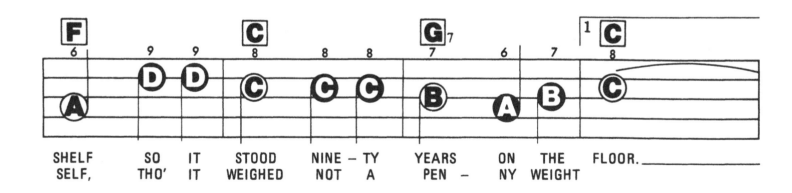

SHELF SO IT STOOD NINE — TY YEARS ON THE FLOOR._____
SELF, THO' IT WEIGHED NOT A PEN — NY WEIGHT

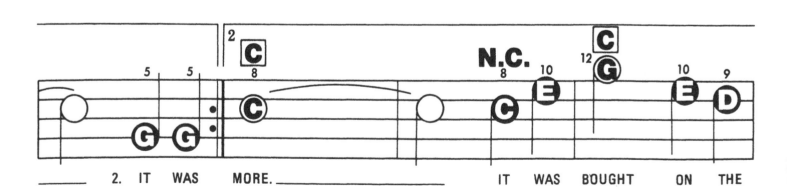

_____ 2. IT WAS MORE._____ IT WAS BOUGHT ON THE

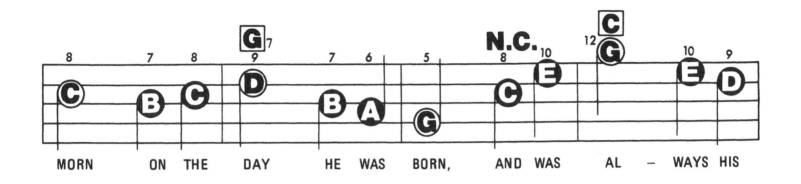

MORN   ON   THE   DAY   HE   WAS   BORN,   AND   WAS   AL – WAYS   HIS

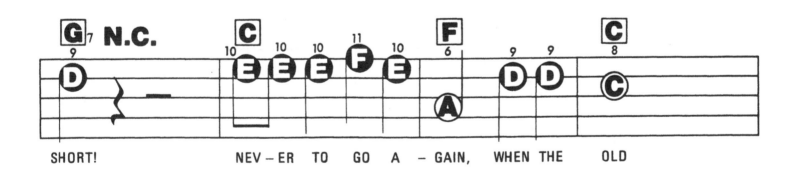

TREAS – URE   AND   PRIDE._____   BUT   IT   STOPPED!

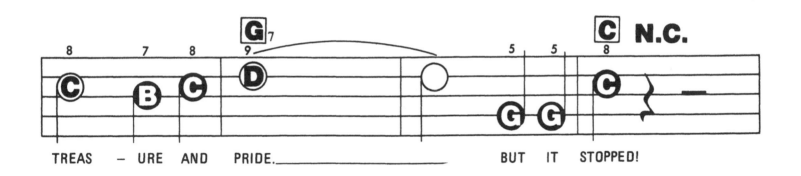

SHORT!   NEV –ER   TO   GO   A – GAIN,   WHEN   THE   OLD

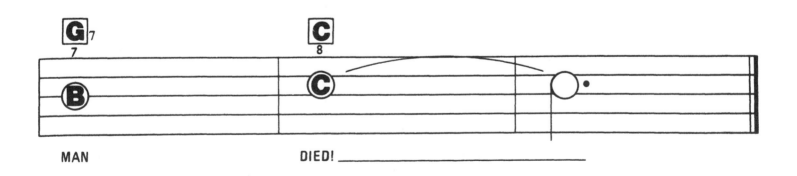

MAN   DIED! _____

JUST A CLOSER WALK WITH THEE

Registration 7
Rhythm: Swing

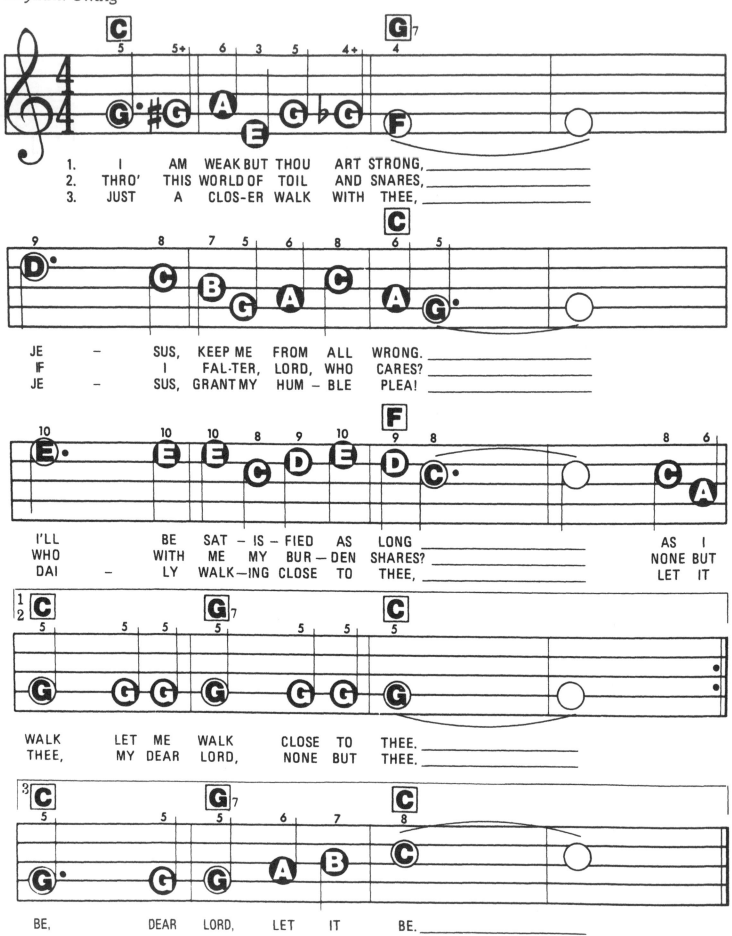

1. I AM WEAK BUT THOU ART STRONG, _____
2. THRO' THIS WORLD OF TOIL AND SNARES, _____
3. JUST A CLOS-ER WALK WITH THEE, _____

JE - SUS, KEEP ME FROM ALL WRONG. _____
IF I FAL-TER, LORD, WHO CARES? _____
JE - SUS, GRANT MY HUM - BLE PLEA! _____

I'LL BE SAT - IS - FIED AS LONG _____ AS I
WHO WITH ME MY BUR - DEN SHARES? _____ NONE BUT
DAI - LY WALK—ING CLOSE TO THEE, _____ LET IT

WALK LET ME WALK CLOSE TO THEE. _____
THEE, MY DEAR WALK LORD, NONE BUT THEE. _____

BE, DEAR LORD, LET IT BE. _____

LA GOLONDRINA

Registration 10
Rhythm: Waltz

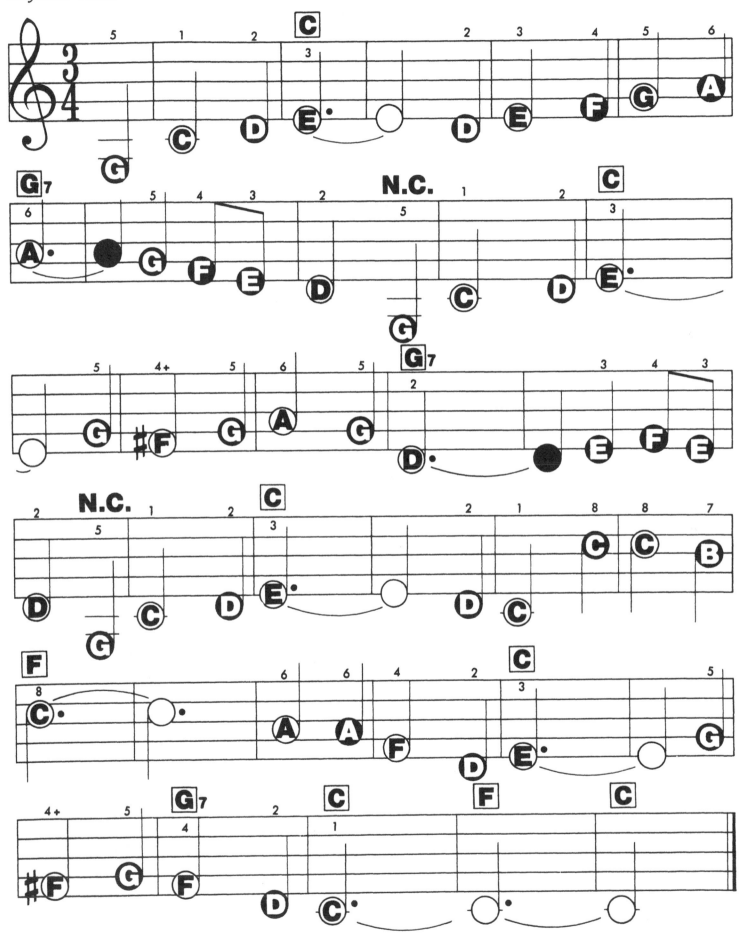

LA PALOMA

Registration 7
Rhythm: Rhumba or Latin

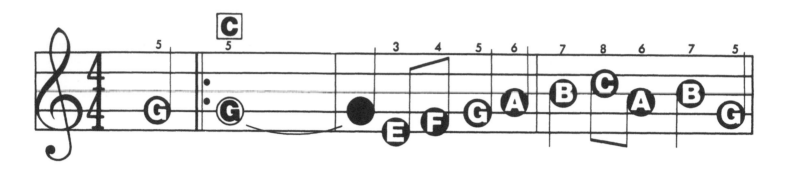

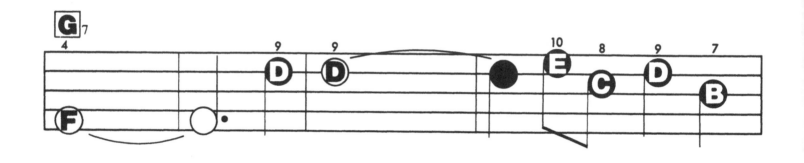

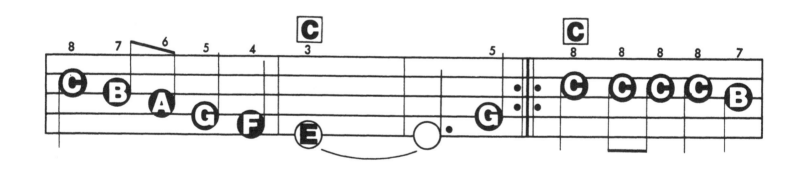

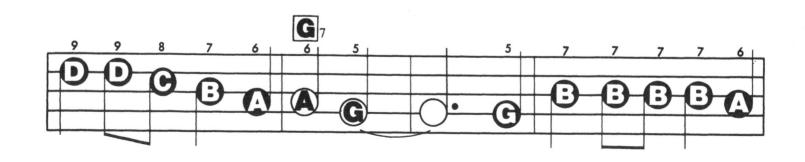

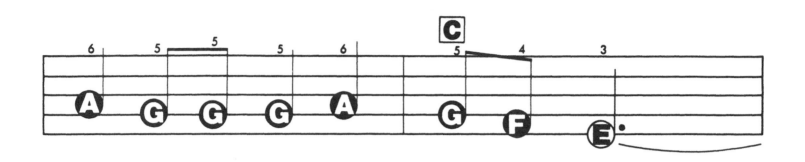

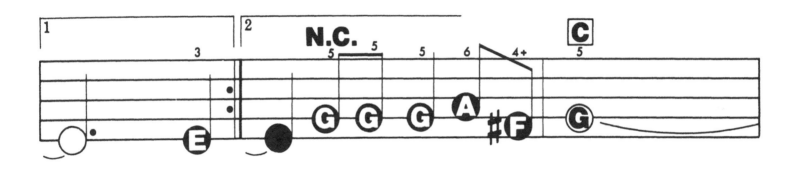

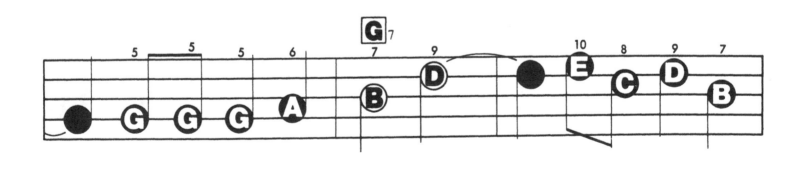

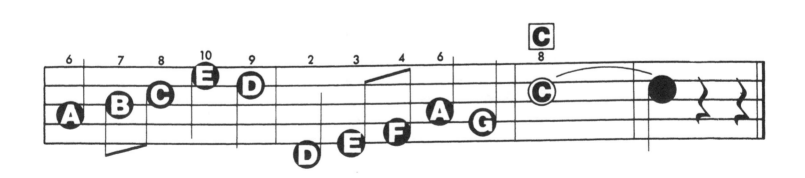

LOCH LOMOND

Registration 1
Rhythm: Fox Trot or Swing

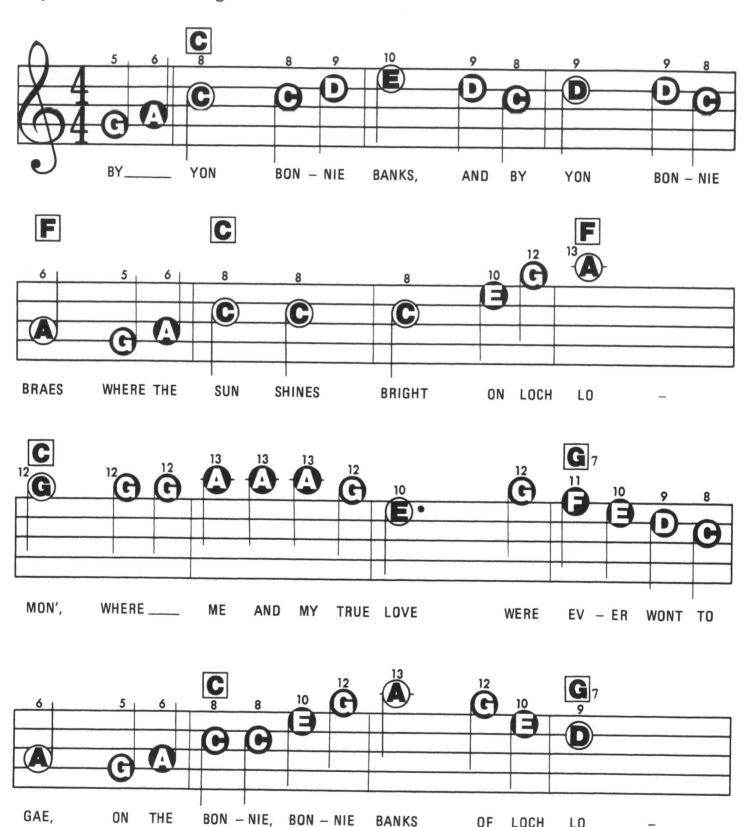

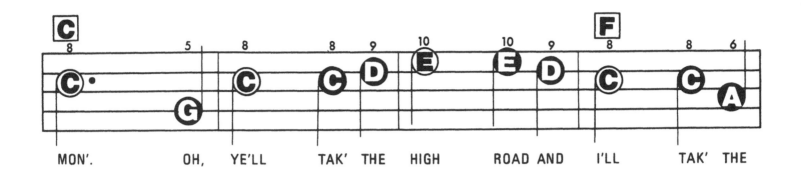

MON'. OH, YE'LL TAK' THE HIGH ROAD AND I'LL TAK' THE

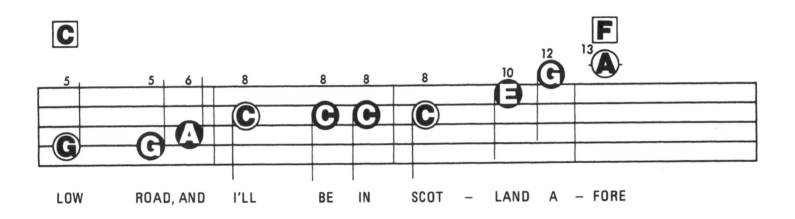

LOW ROAD, AND I'LL BE IN SCOT — LAND A — FORE

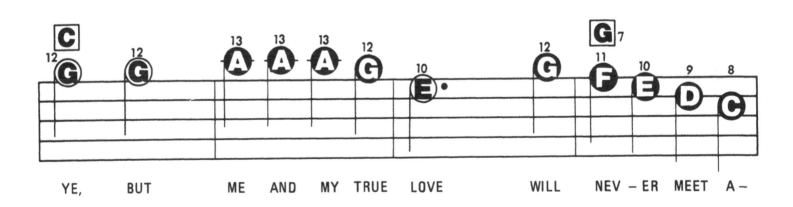

YE, BUT ME AND MY TRUE LOVE WILL NEV — ER MEET A—

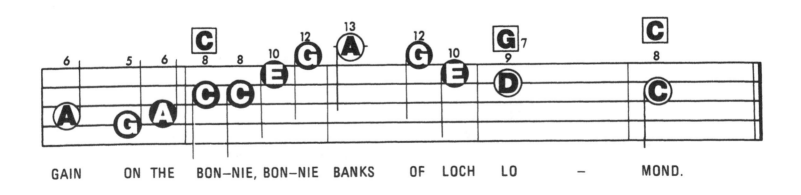

GAIN ON THE BON—NIE, BON—NIE BANKS OF LOCH LO — MOND.

LULLABY

Registration 10
Rhythm: Waltz

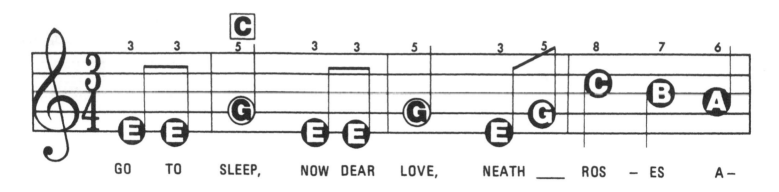

GO TO SLEEP, NOW DEAR LOVE, NEATH ___ ROS - ES A-

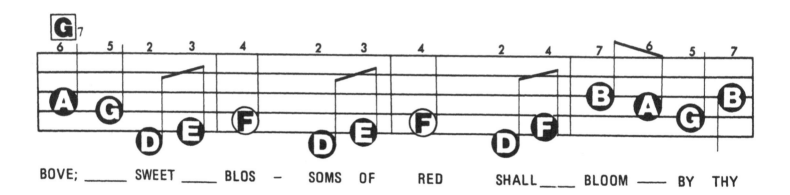

BOVE; ___ SWEET ___ BLOS - SOMS OF RED SHALL___ BLOOM ___ BY THY

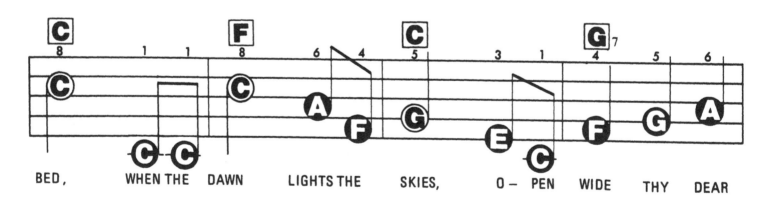

BED, WHEN THE DAWN LIGHTS THE SKIES, O - PEN WIDE THY DEAR

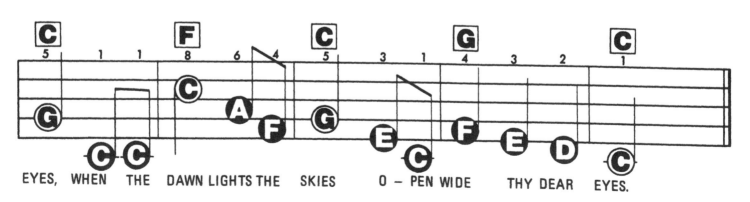

EYES, WHEN THE DAWN LIGHTS THE SKIES O - PEN WIDE THY DEAR EYES.

MIGHTY LAK' A ROSE

Registration 2
Rhythm: Fox Trot or Swing

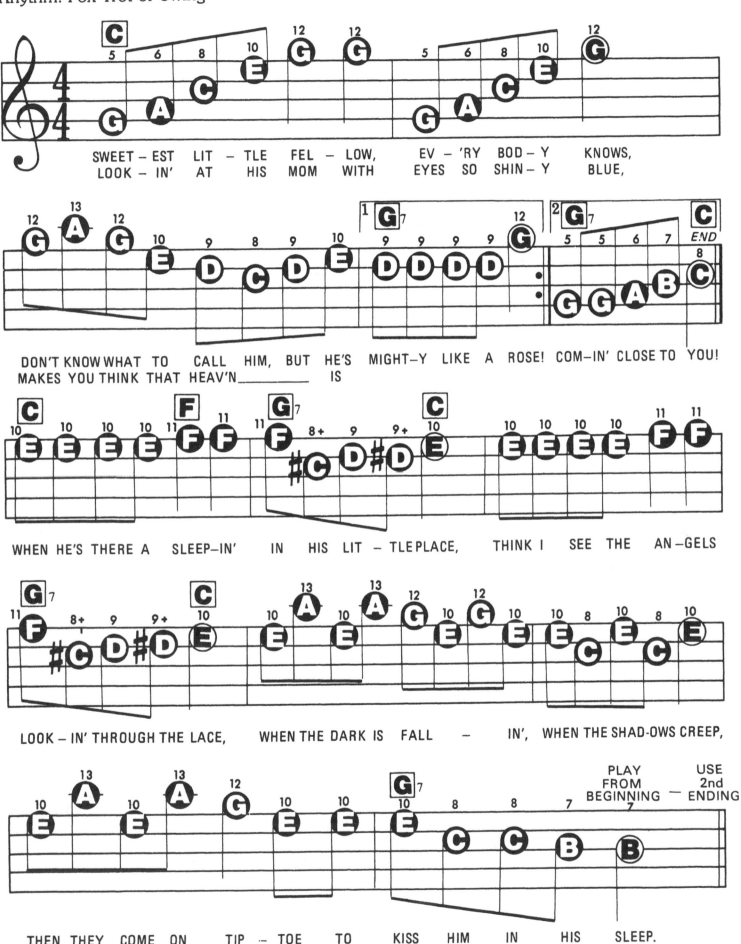

THE MARINE'S HYMN

Registration 9
Rhythm: March or Polka

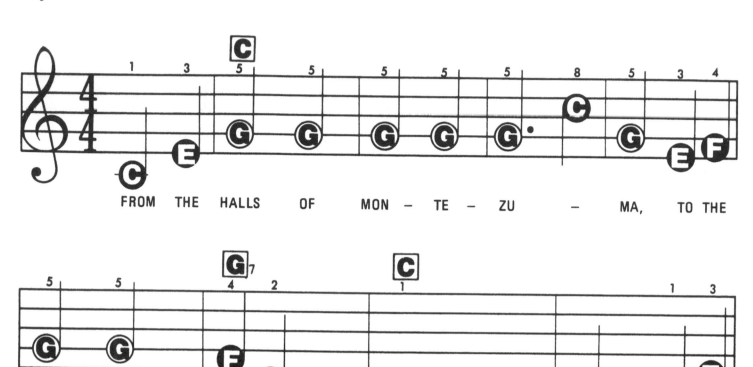

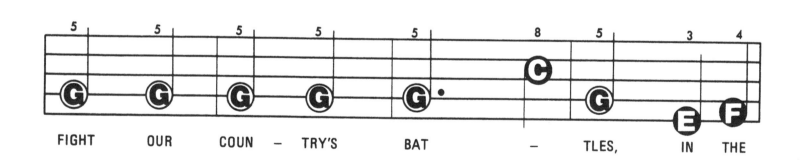

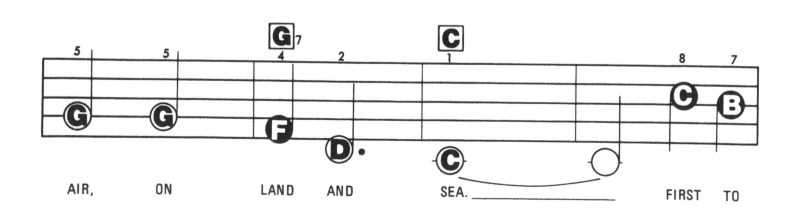

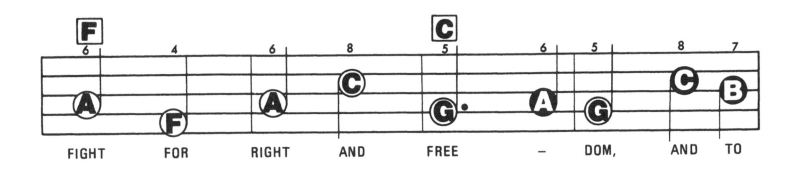

FIGHT   FOR   RIGHT   AND   FREE   —   DOM,   AND   TO

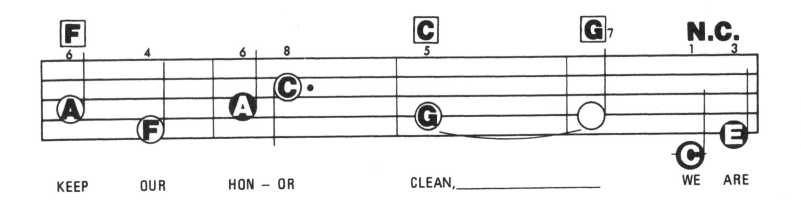

KEEP   OUR   HON – OR   CLEAN,_____   WE ARE

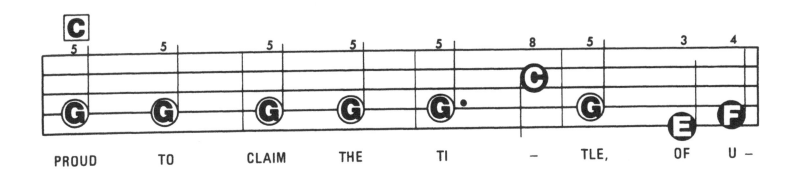

PROUD   TO   CLAIM   THE   TI   —   TLE,   OF   U –

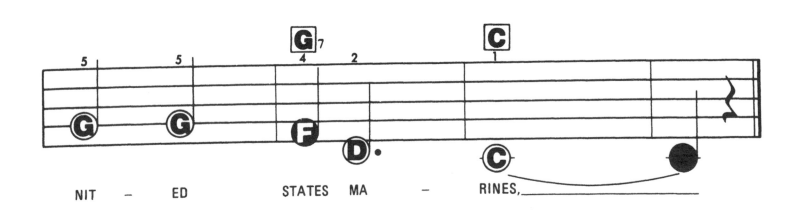

NIT – ED   STATES MA   —   RINES,_____

MY OLD KENTUCKY HOME

Registration 8
Rhythm: Fox Trot or Swing

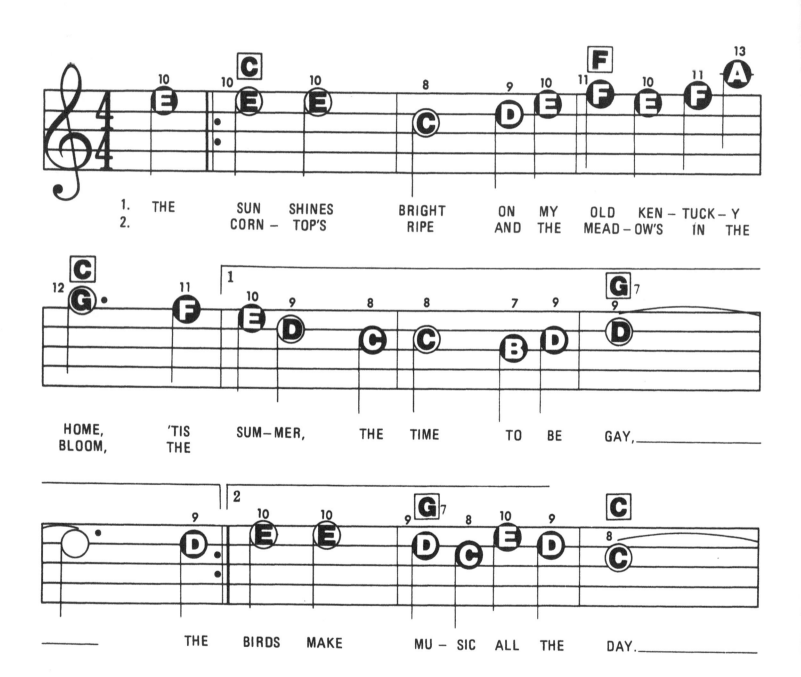

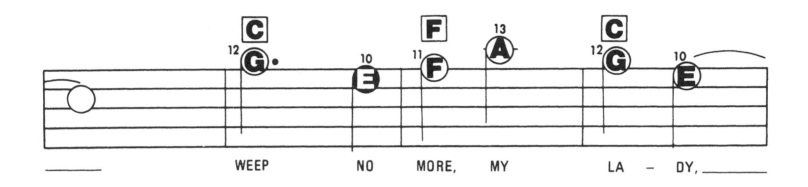

WEEP   NO   MORE,   MY   LA - DY,

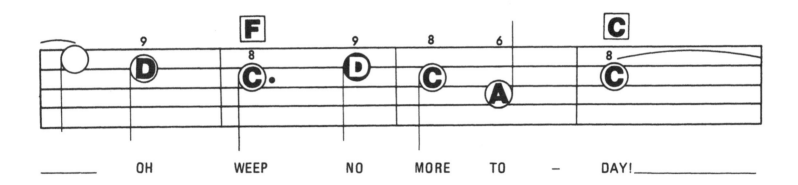

OH   WEEP   NO   MORE   TO - DAY!

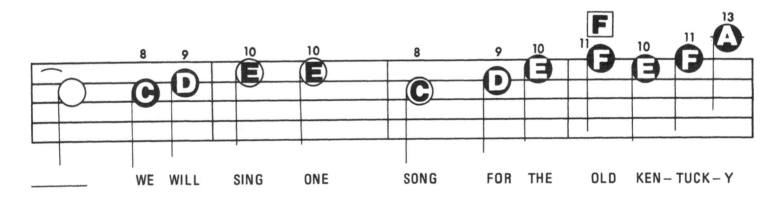

WE   WILL   SING   ONE   SONG   FOR   THE   OLD   KEN – TUCK – Y

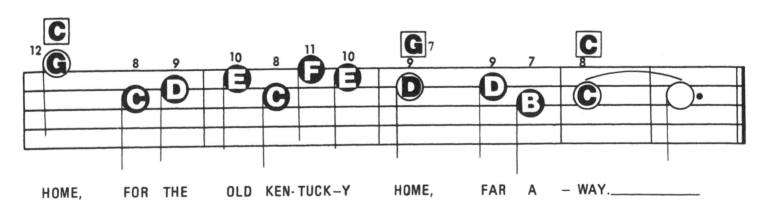

HOME,   FOR   THE   OLD   KEN - TUCK - Y   HOME,   FAR   A - WAY.

ODE TO JOY

Registration 2
Rhythm: Rock or 8 Beat

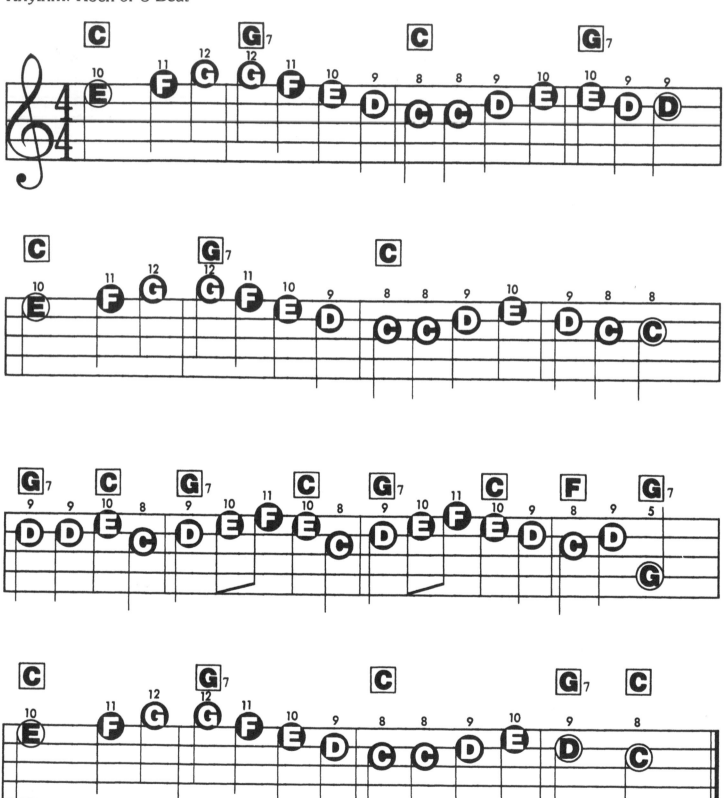

POMP AND CIRCUMSTANCE

Registration 9
Rhythm: Fox Trot or Swing

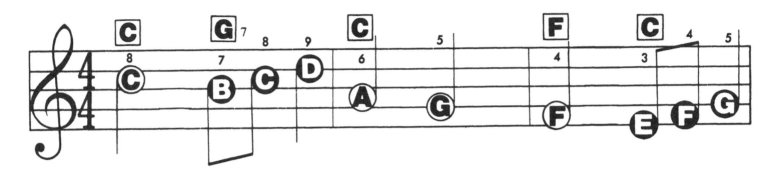

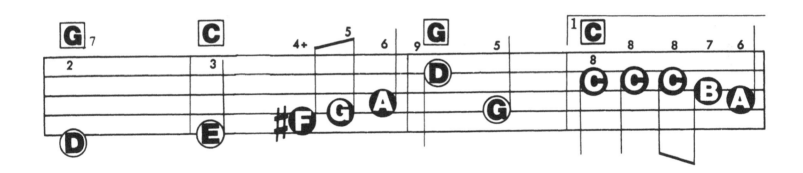

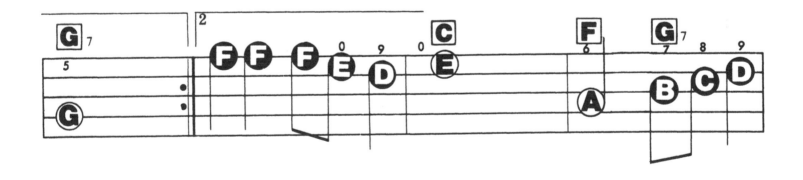

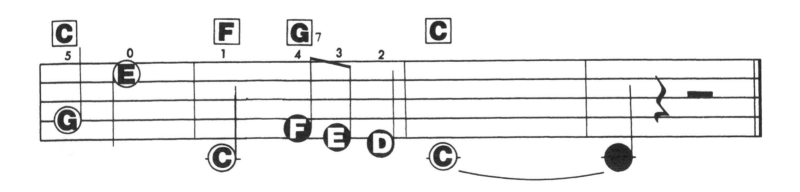

OH SUSANNA

Registration 4
Rhythm: Fox Trot or Swing

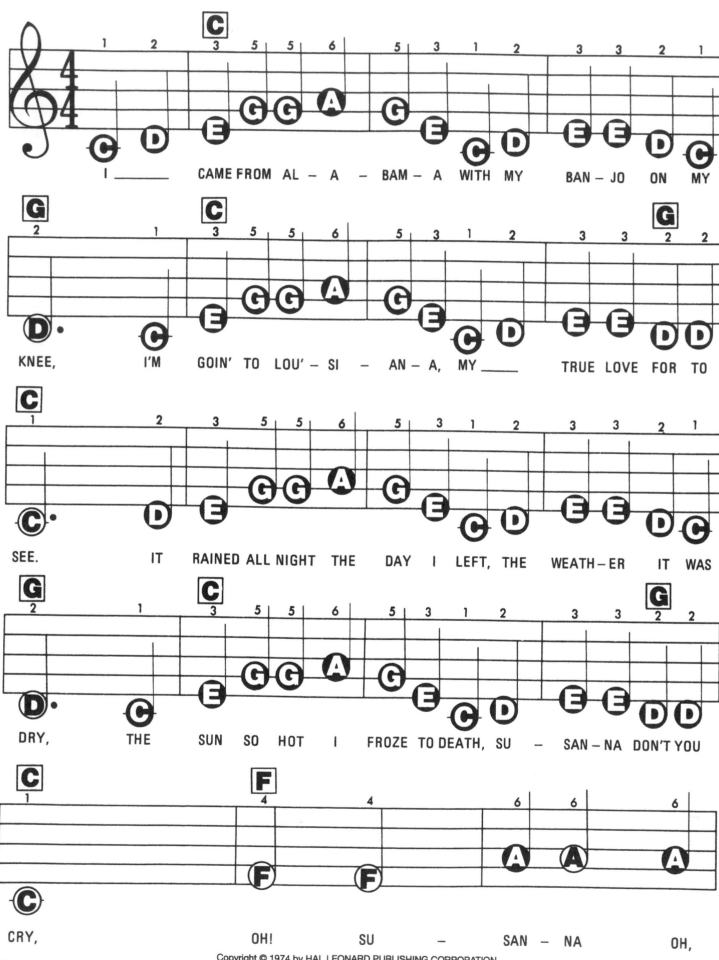

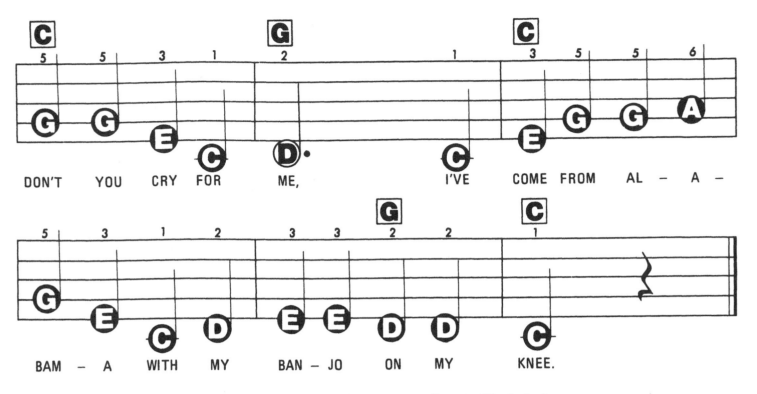

DON'T YOU CRY FOR ME, I'VE COME FROM AL - A -

BAM - A WITH MY BAN - JO ON MY KNEE.

WABASH CANNON BALL

Registration 7
Rhythm: Fox Trot or Swing

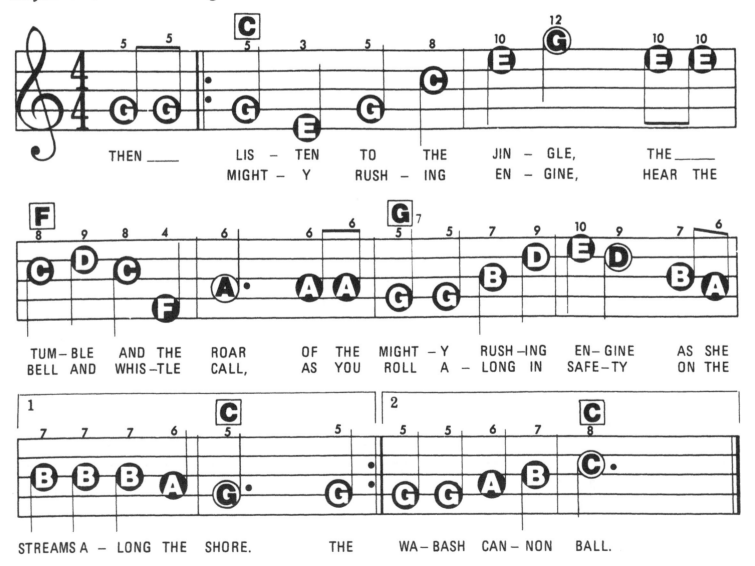

THEN _____ LIS - TEN TO THE JIN - GLE, THE _____
MIGHT - Y RUSH - ING EN - GINE, HEAR THE

TUM - BLE AND THE ROAR OF THE MIGHT - Y RUSH-ING EN-GINE AS SHE
BELL AND WHIS-TLE CALL, AS YOU ROLL A - LONG IN SAFE-TY ON THE

STREAMS A - LONG THE SHORE. THE WA - BASH CAN - NON BALL.

OH, THEM GOLDEN SLIPPERS

Registration 8
Rhythm: Fox Trot or Swing

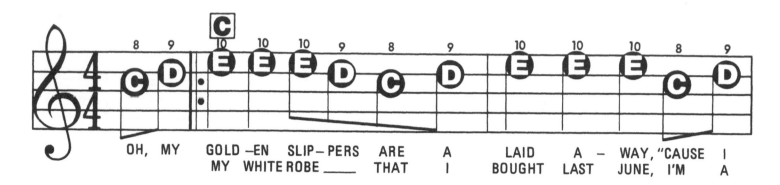

OH, MY GOLD—EN SLIP—PERS ARE A LAID A—WAY, "CAUSE I
MY WHITE ROBE ____ THAT I BOUGHT LAST JUNE, I'M A

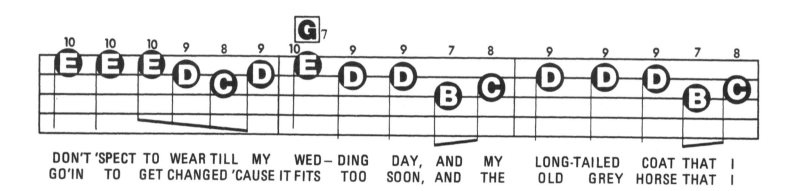

DON'T 'SPECT TO WEAR TILL MY WED—DING DAY, AND MY LONG-TAILED COAT THAT I
GO'IN TO GET CHANGED 'CAUSE IT FITS TOO SOON, AND THE OLD GREY HORSE THAT I

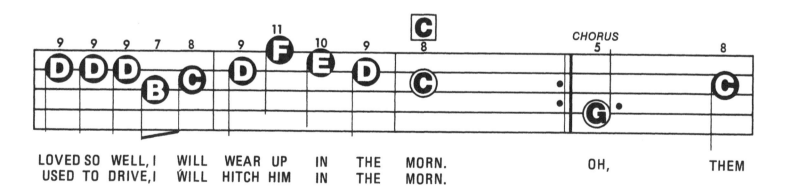

LOVED SO WELL, I WILL WEAR UP IN THE MORN.
USED TO DRIVE, I WILL HITCH HIM IN THE MORN. OH, THEM

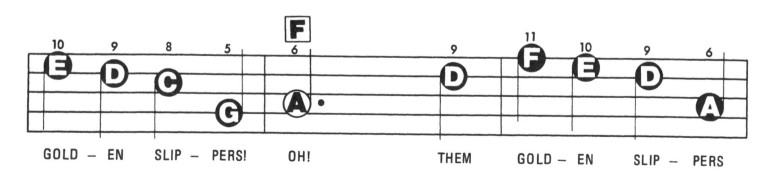

GOLD—EN SLIP—PERS! OH! THEM GOLD—EN SLIP—PERS

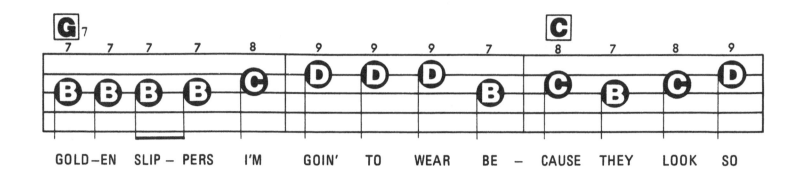

GOLD–EN SLIP–PERS I'M GOIN' TO WEAR BE – CAUSE THEY LOOK SO

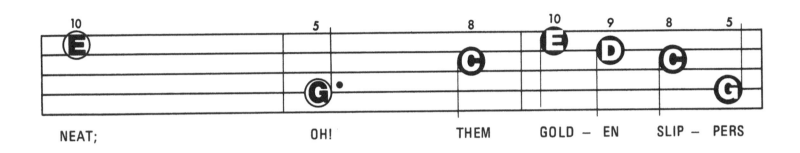

NEAT; OH! THEM GOLD – EN SLIP – PERS

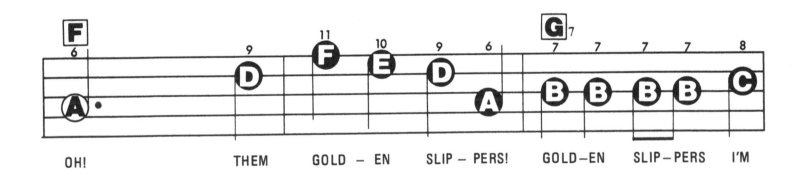

OH! THEM GOLD – EN SLIP – PERS! GOLD–EN SLIP–PERS I'M

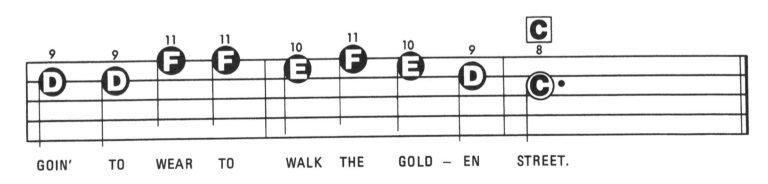

GOIN' TO WEAR TO WALK THE GOLD – EN STREET.

2. OH, MY OLD BANJO HANGS ON THE WALL, 'CAUSE IT HASN'T BEEN TUNED SINCE WAY LAST FALL,
BUT THE FOLKS ALL SAY WE WILL HAVE A GOOD TIME, WHEN WE RIDE UP IN THE CHARIOT IN THE MORN.
THERE'S OLD BROTHER BEN AND SISTER LUCE, THEY WILL TELEGRAPH THE NEWS TO UNCLE BACCO JOE,
WHAT A GREAT CAMP–MEETING THERE WILL BE THAT DAY, WHEN WE RIDE UP IN THE CHARIOT IN THE MORN.
CHORUS

3. SO, IT'S GOOD–BYE CHILDREN, I WILL HAVE TO GO,
WHERE THE RAIN DOESN'T FALL OR THE WIND DOESN'T BLOW, AND YOUR ULSTER COATS, WHY, YOU WILL NOT NEED,
WHEN YOU RIDE UP IN THE CHARIOT IN THE MORN.
BUT YOUR GOLDEN SLIPPERS MUST BE NEAT AND CLEAN, AND YOUR AGE MUST BE JUST SWEET SIXTEEN,
AND YOUR WHITE KID GLOVES, YOU WILL HAVE TO WEAR, WHEN YOU RIDE UP IN THE CHARIOT, IN THE MORN.
CHORUS

ON TOP OF OLD SMOKEY

Registration 2
Rhythm: Waltz

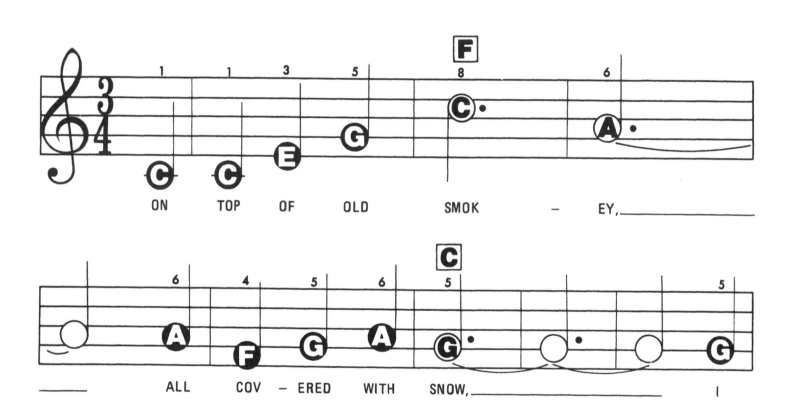

ON TOP OF OLD SMOK — EY,_____ ALL COV — ERED WITH SNOW,_____ I

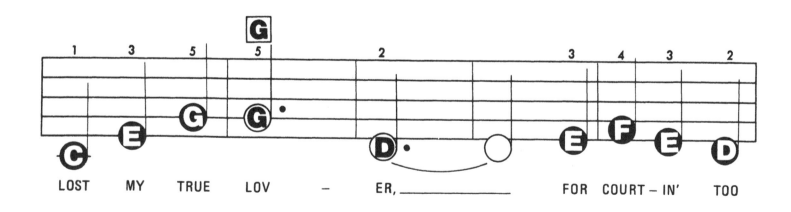

LOST MY TRUE LOV — ER,_____ FOR COURT — IN' TOO

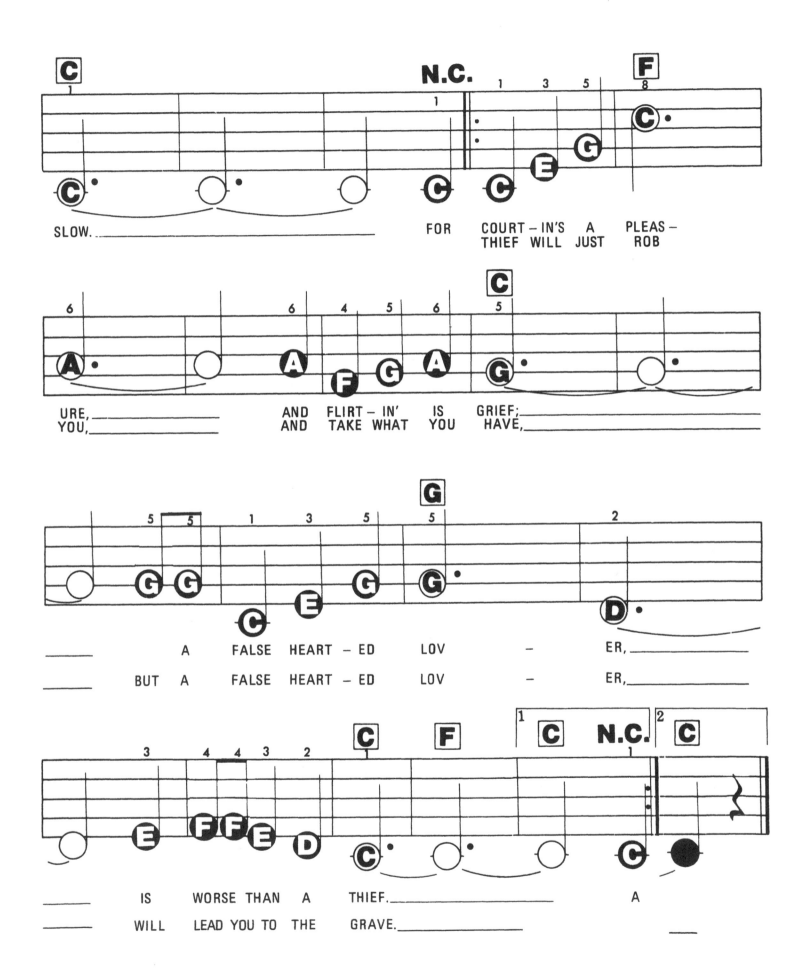

OVER THE WAVES
(Popular version known as LOVELIEST NIGHT OF THE YEAR)

Registration 1
Rhythm: Waltz

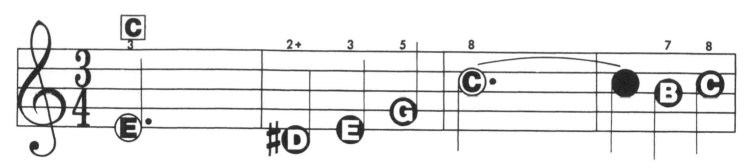

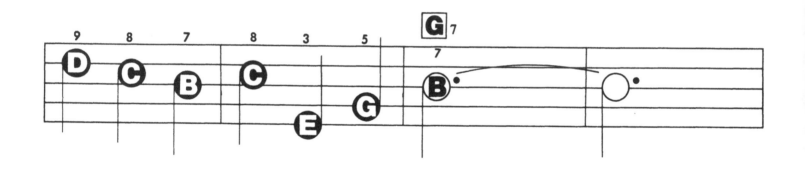

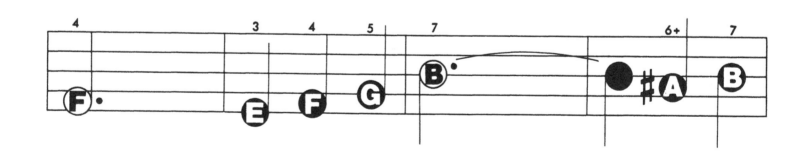

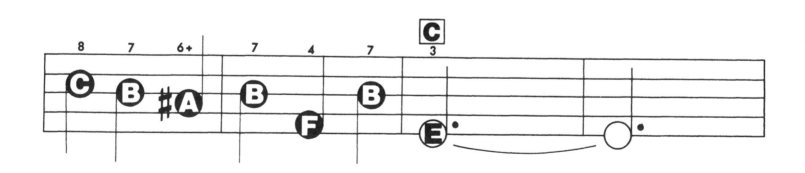

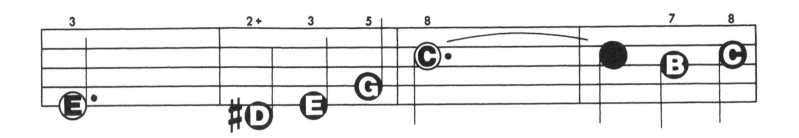

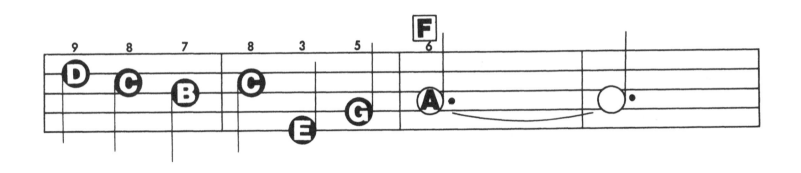

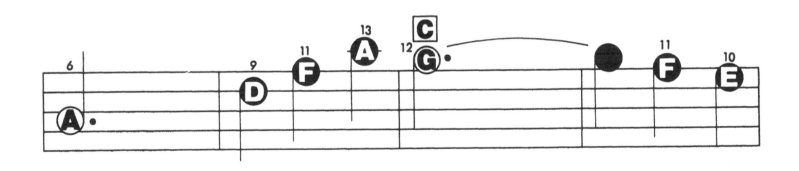

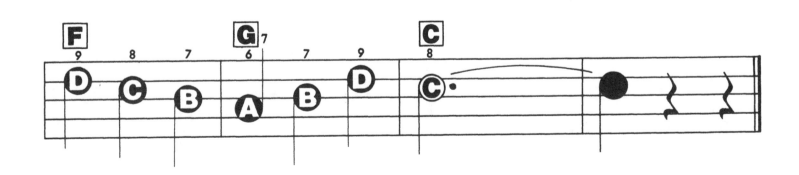

67

RED RIVER VALLEY

Registration 4
Rhythm: Waltz

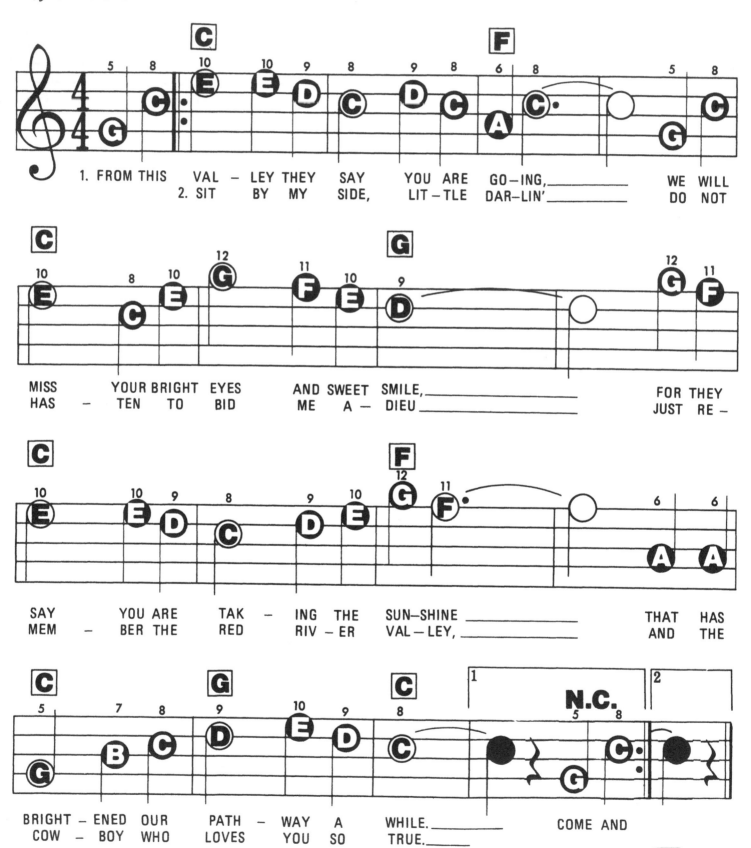

SHENANDOAH

Registration 2
Rhythm: Fox Trot or Swing

1. OH, SHEN – AN – DOAH ____ I LOVE YOUR DAUGH – TER
2. SHEN – AN – DOAH ____ GIVE ME YOUR DAUGH – TER

CROSS ____ THE ROLL-ING RIV – ER OH!
SHEN - AN – DOAH ___ GAZE O'ER THE
MA – NY YEARS ___ I'VE STAYED TO

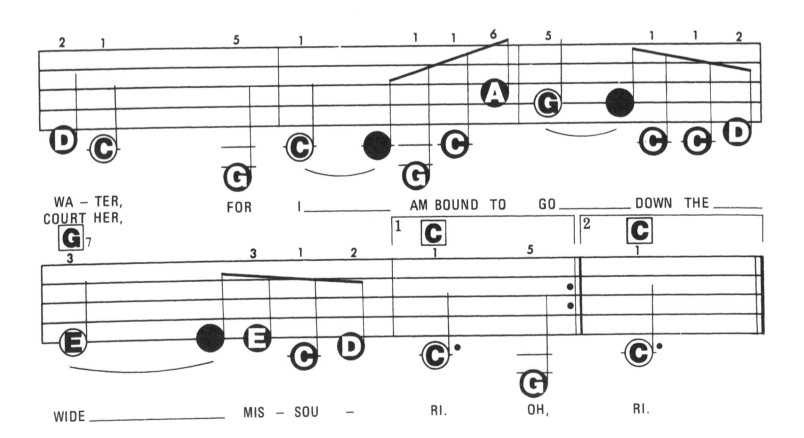

WA – TER, FOR I ____ AM BOUND TO GO ____ DOWN THE ____
COURT HER,

WIDE ____ MIS – SOU – RI. OH, RI.

SCOTLAND THE BRAVE

Registration 9
Rhythm: March

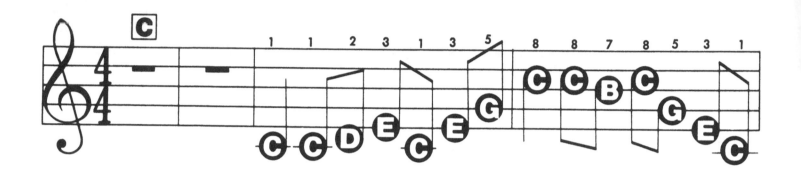

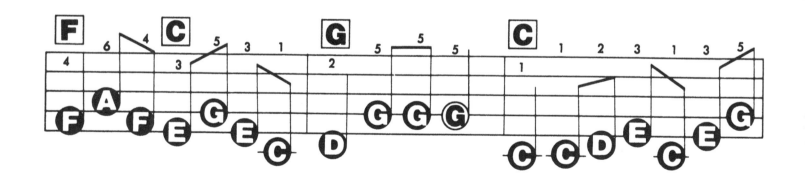

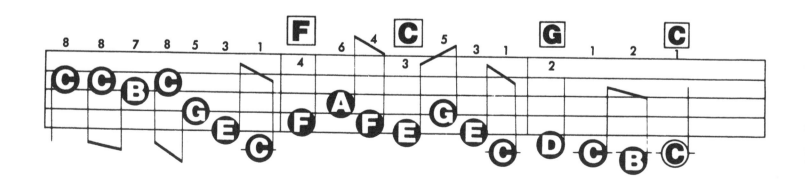

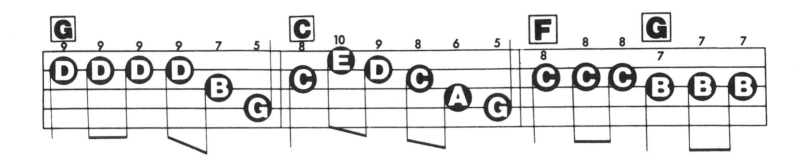

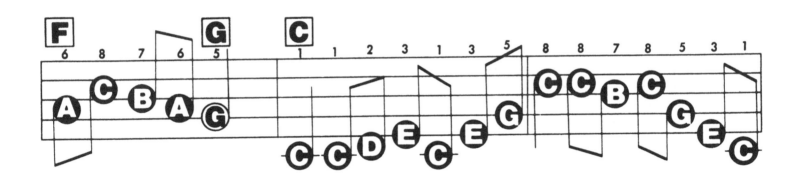

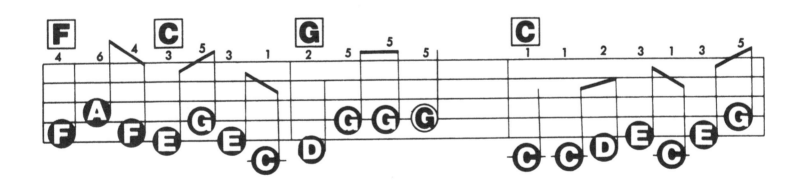

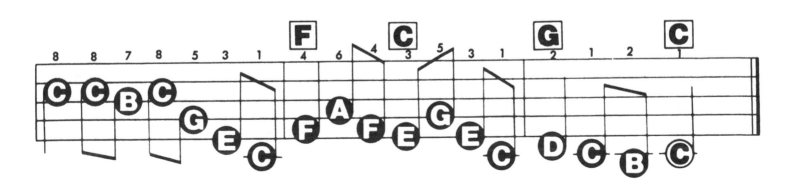

SILVER THREADS AMONG THE GOLD

Registration 8
Rhythm: Fox Trot or Swing

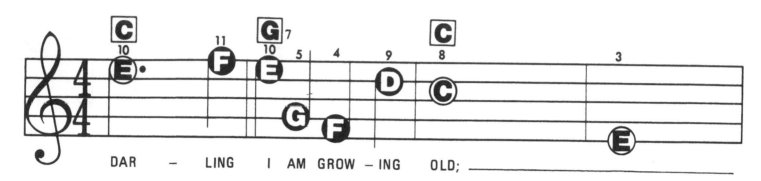

DAR — LING   I AM GROW — ING   OLD; _____

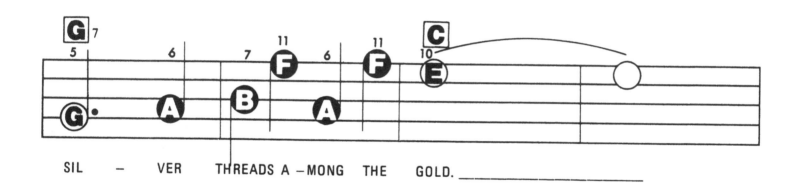

SIL — VER   THREADS A —MONG   THE   GOLD. _____

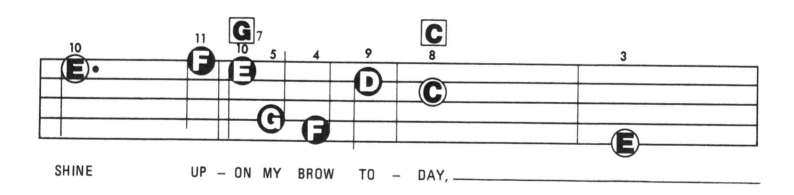

SHINE   UP — ON MY BROW TO — DAY, _____

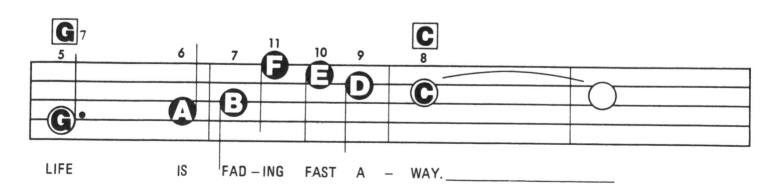

LIFE   IS FAD — ING FAST A — WAY. _____

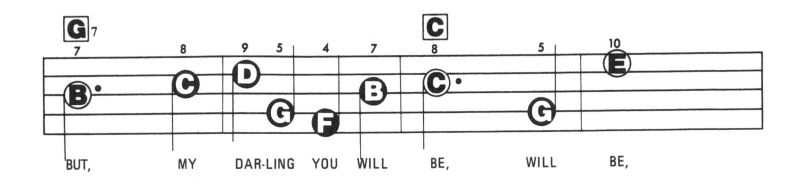

BUT,   MY   DAR-LING YOU WILL   BE,   WILL   BE,

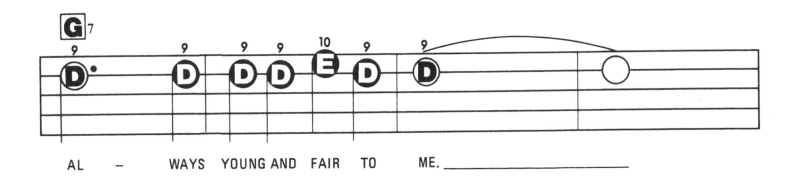

AL   —   WAYS YOUNG AND FAIR   TO   ME.

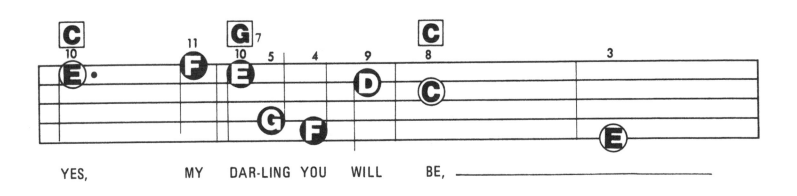

YES,   MY   DAR-LING YOU   WILL   BE,

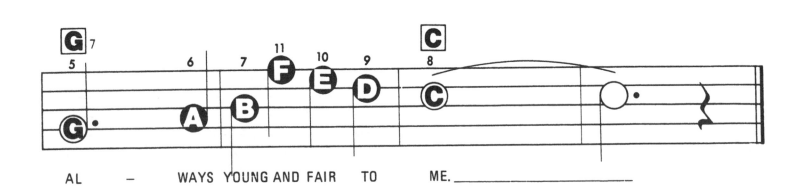

AL   —   WAYS YOUNG AND FAIR   TO   ME.

TALES OF THE VIENNA WOODS

Registration 3
Rhythm: Waltz

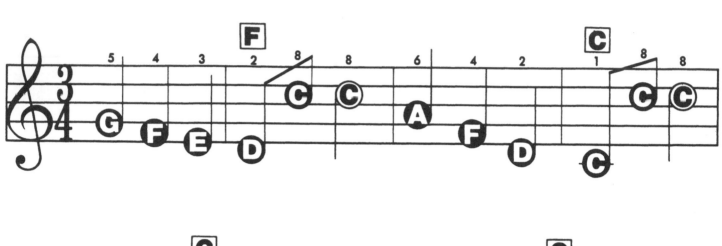

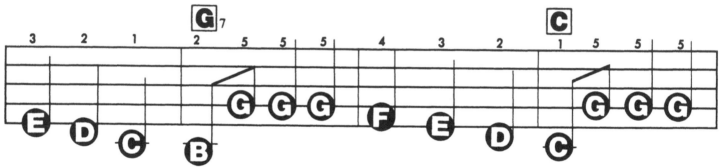

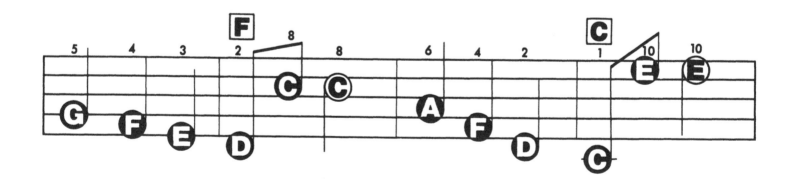

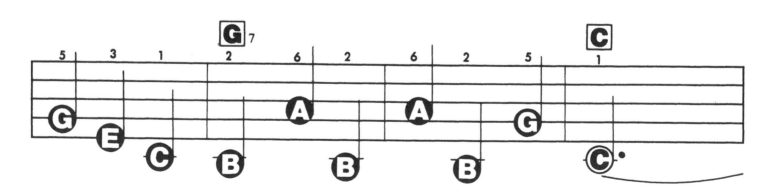

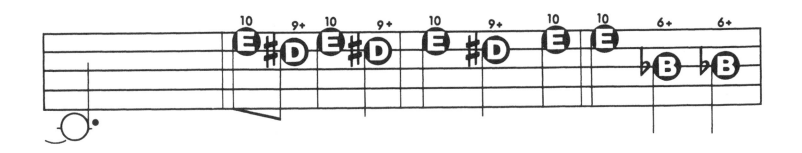

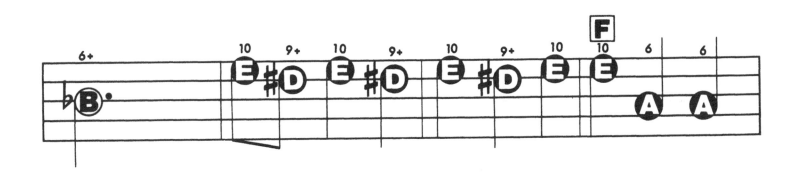

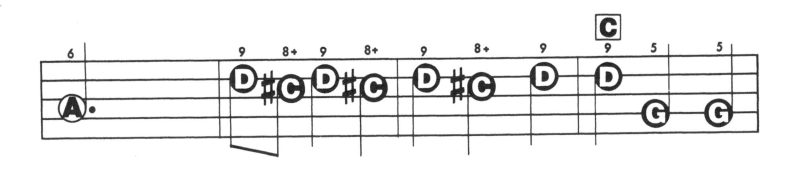

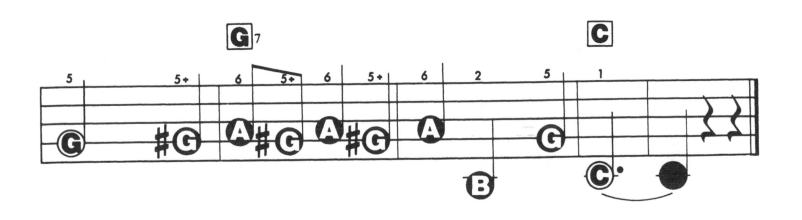

TA-RA-RA BOOM-DER-E

Registration 4
Rhythm: March or Fox Trot

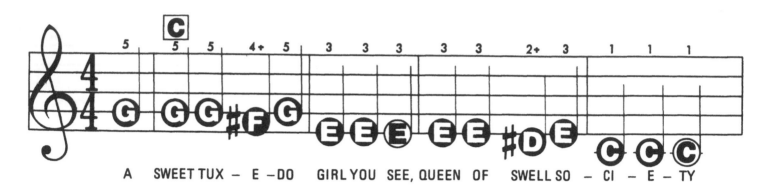

A SWEET TUX – E –DO GIRL YOU SEE, QUEEN OF SWELL SO – CI – E – TY

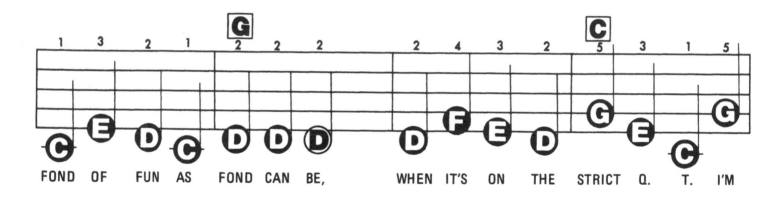

FOND OF FUN AS FOND CAN BE, WHEN IT'S ON THE STRICT Q. T. I'M

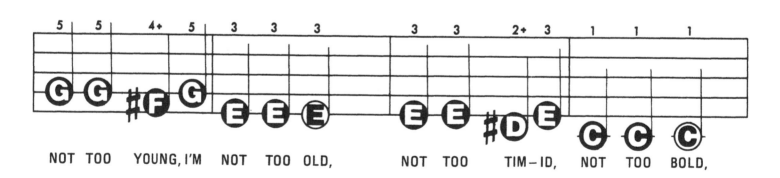

NOT TOO YOUNG, I'M NOT TOO OLD, NOT TOO TIM–ID, NOT TOO BOLD,

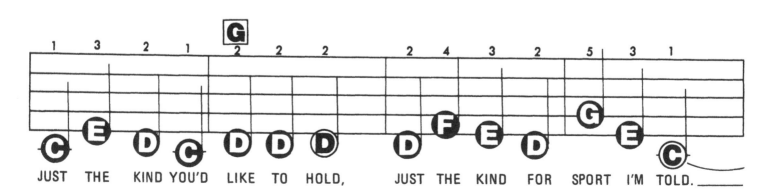

JUST THE KIND YOU'D LIKE TO HOLD, JUST THE KIND FOR SPORT I'M TOLD.

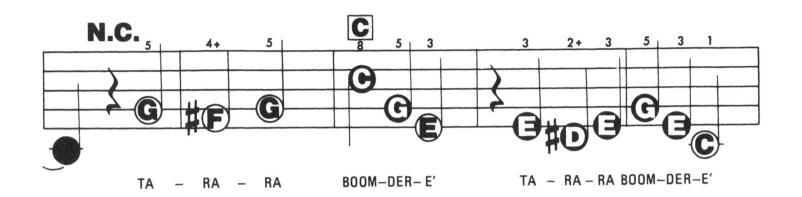

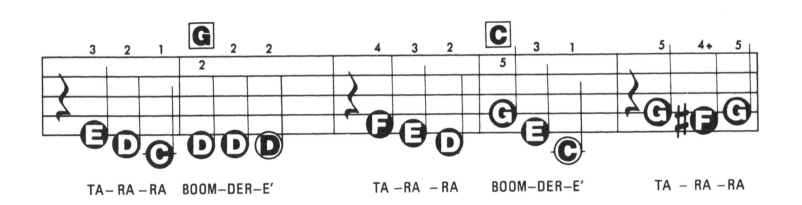

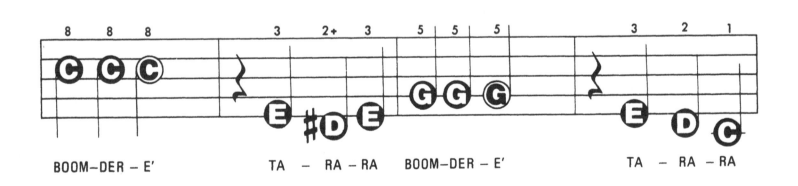

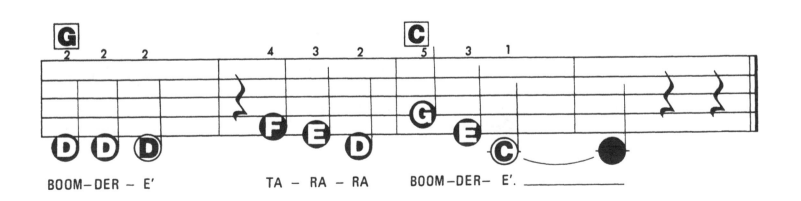

THERE IS A TAVERN IN THE TOWN

Registration 5
Rhythm: Fox Trot or Swing

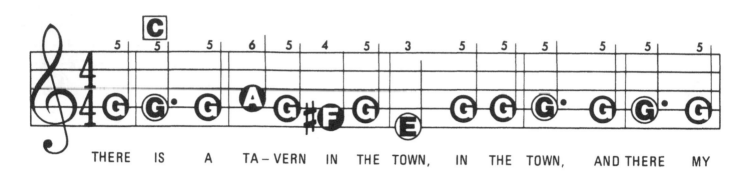

THERE IS A TA–VERN IN THE TOWN, IN THE TOWN, AND THERE MY

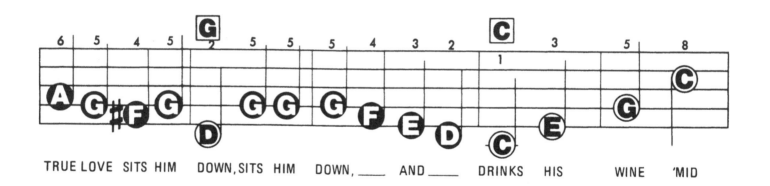

TRUE LOVE SITS HIM DOWN, SITS HIM DOWN, ___ AND ___ DRINKS HIS WINE 'MID

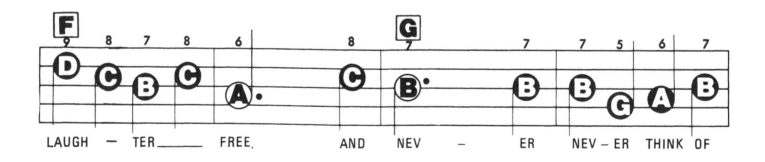

LAUGH — TER ___ FREE, AND NEV – ER NEV–ER THINK OF

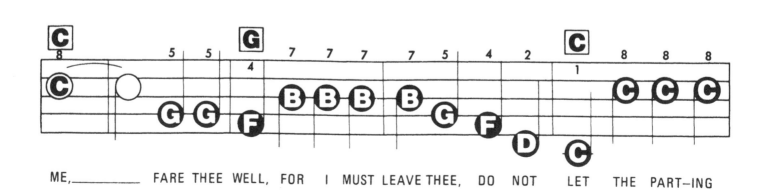

ME, ___ FARE THEE WELL, FOR I MUST LEAVE THEE, DO NOT LET THE PART–ING

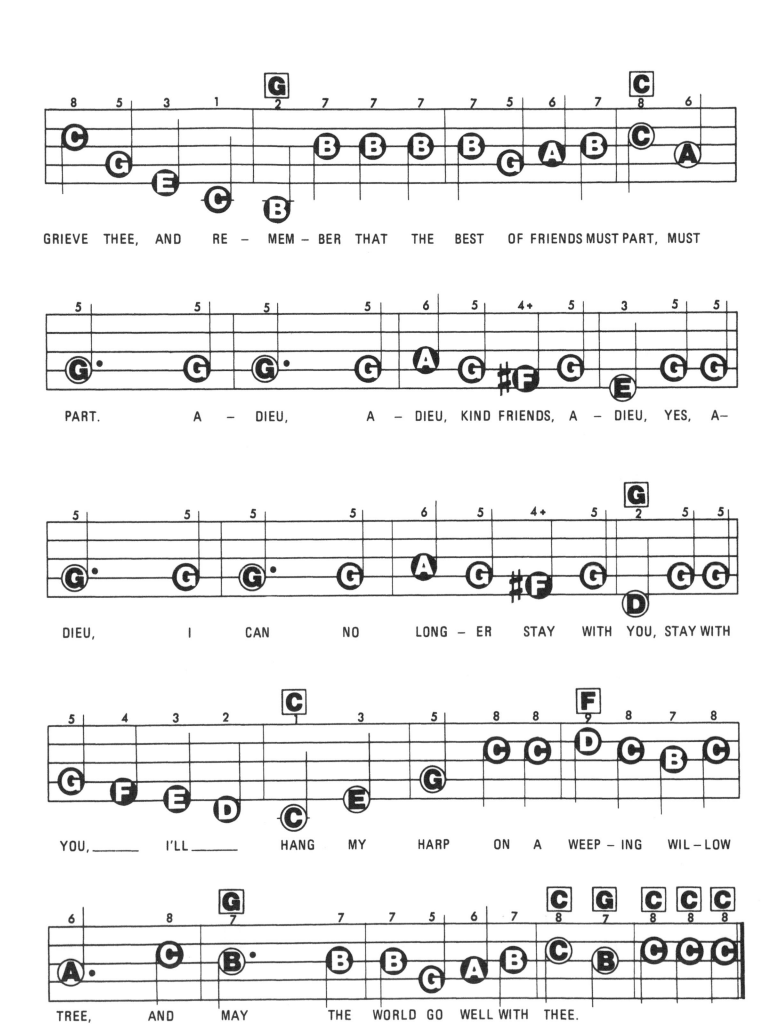

UNDER THE DOUBLE EAGLE

Registration 9
Rhythm: March

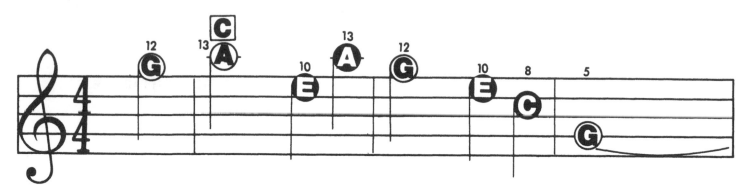

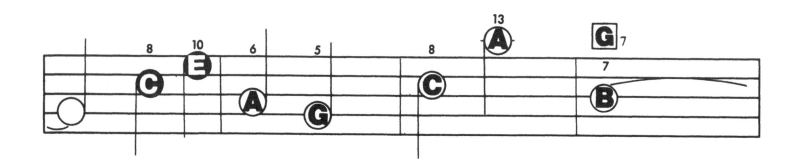

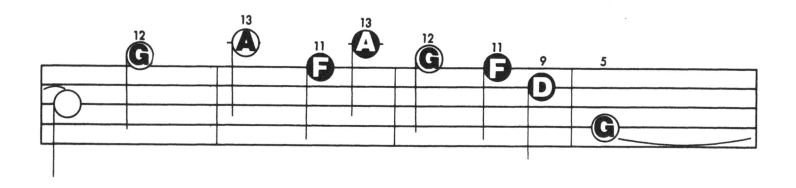

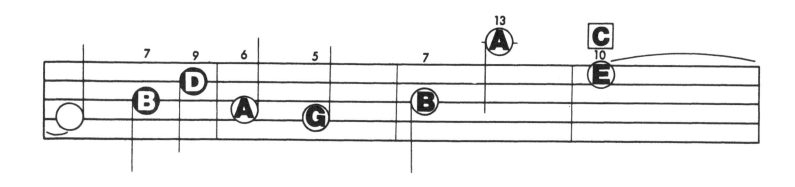

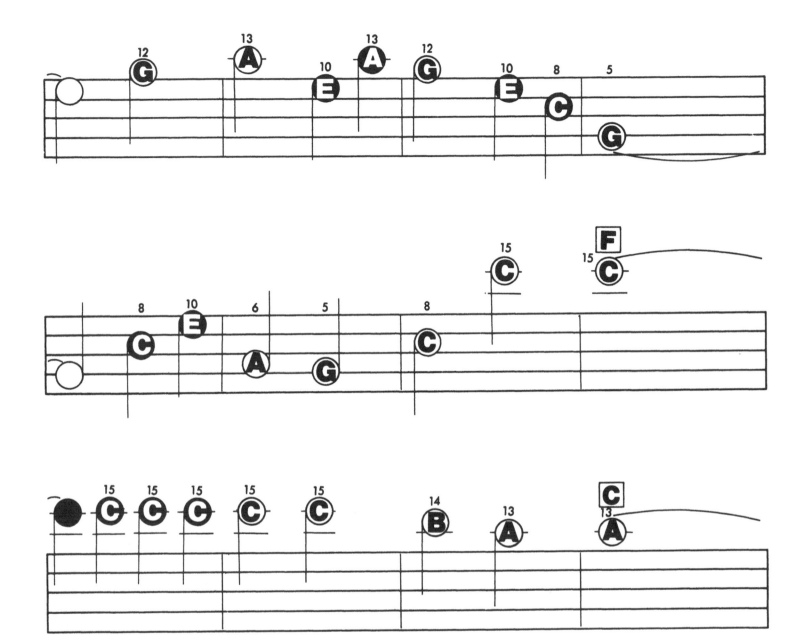

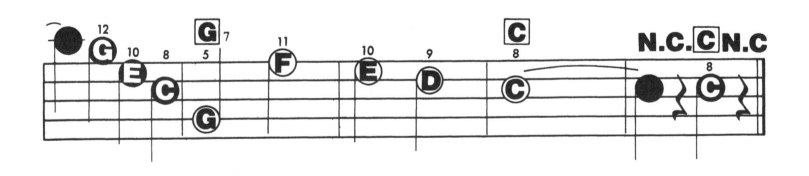

VIENNA LIFE

Registration 3
Rhythm: Waltz

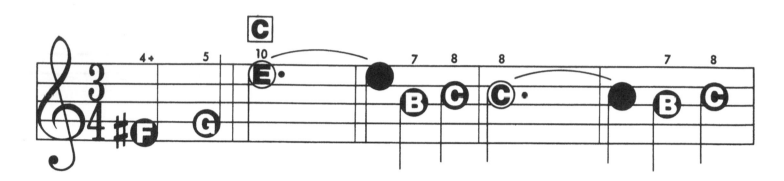

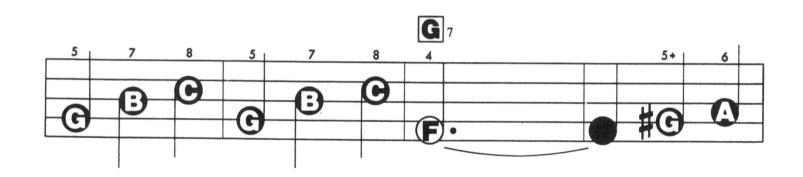

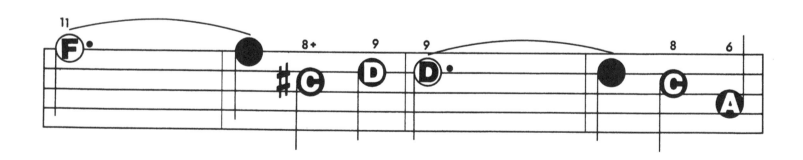

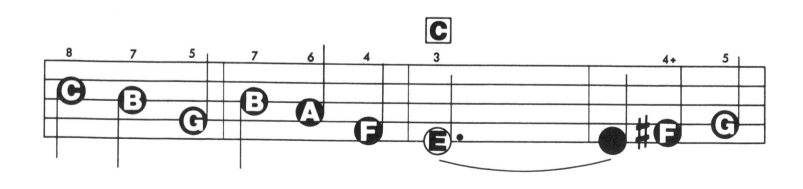

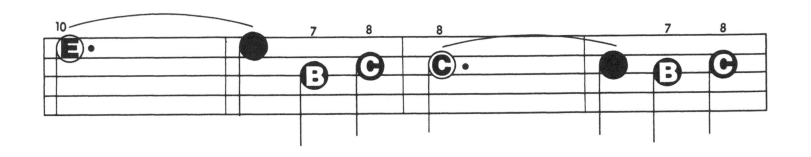

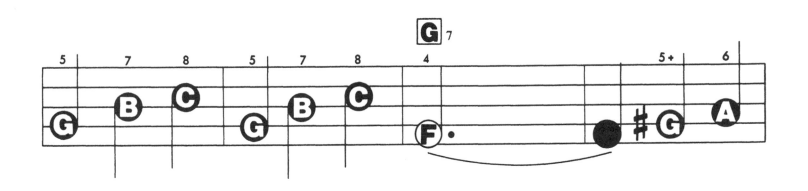

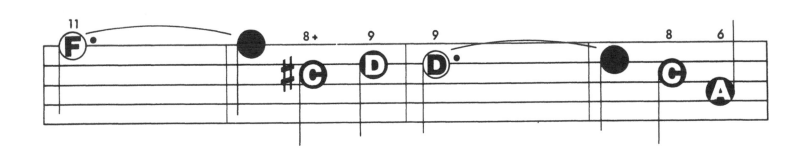

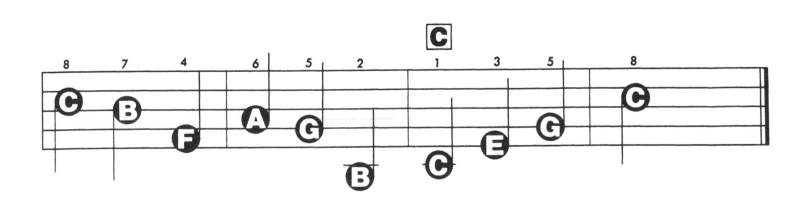

VIVE LA COMPAGNIE

Registration 5
Rhythm: Waltz

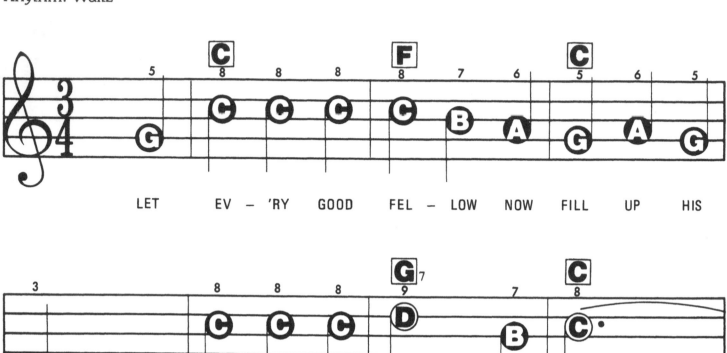

LET   EV — 'RY   GOOD   FEL — LOW   NOW   FILL   UP   HIS

GLASS,   VI — VE   LA   COM — PAGN — IE,____

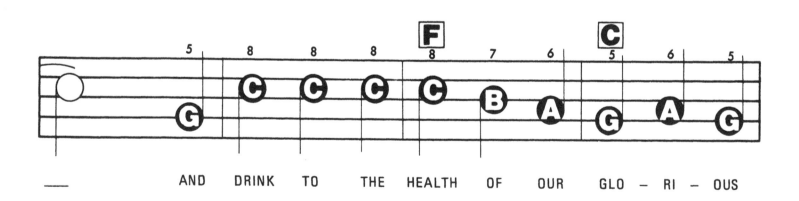

—   AND   DRINK   TO   THE   HEALTH   OF   OUR   GLO — RI — OUS

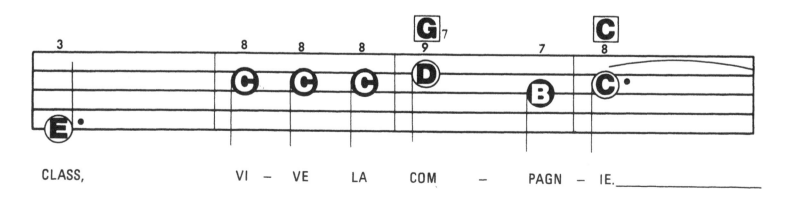

CLASS,   VI — VE   LA   COM — PAGN — IE.____

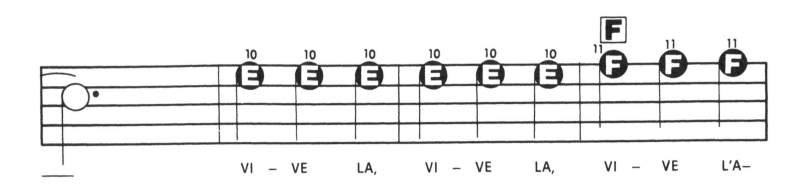

VI — VE LA, VI — VE LA, VI — VE L'A—

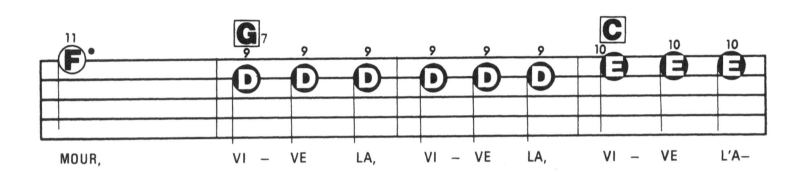

MOUR, VI — VE LA, VI — VE LA, VI — VE L'A—

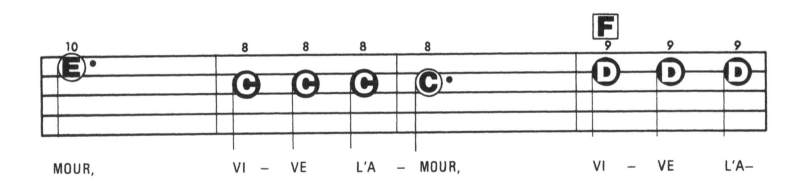

MOUR, VI — VE L'A — MOUR, VI — VE L'A—

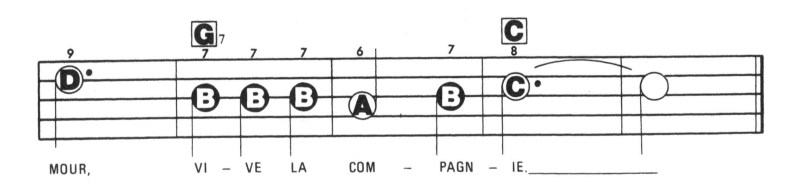

MOUR, VI — VE LA COM — PAGN — IE._____

2. Let every married man drink to his wife,
   Vive la Compagnie,
   The joy of his bosom, the plague of his life,
   Vive la Compagnie
   Vive la, vive la, vive l'amour, etc.

3. Come fill up your glasses, I'll give you a toast,
   Vive la Compagnie,
   Here's health to our good friend our kind worthy host,
   Vive la Compagnie.
   Vive la, vive la, vive l'amour, etc.

WHEN YOU WERE SWEET SIXTEEN

Registration 3
Rhythm: Fox Trot or Swing

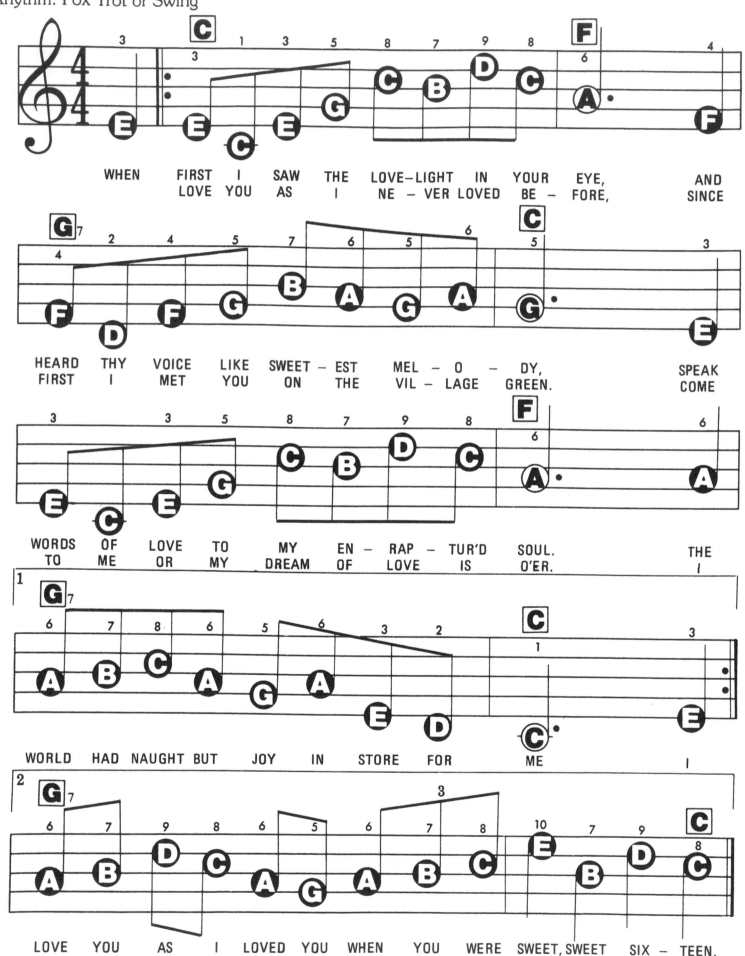

YANKEE DOODLE

Registration 9
Rhythm: March

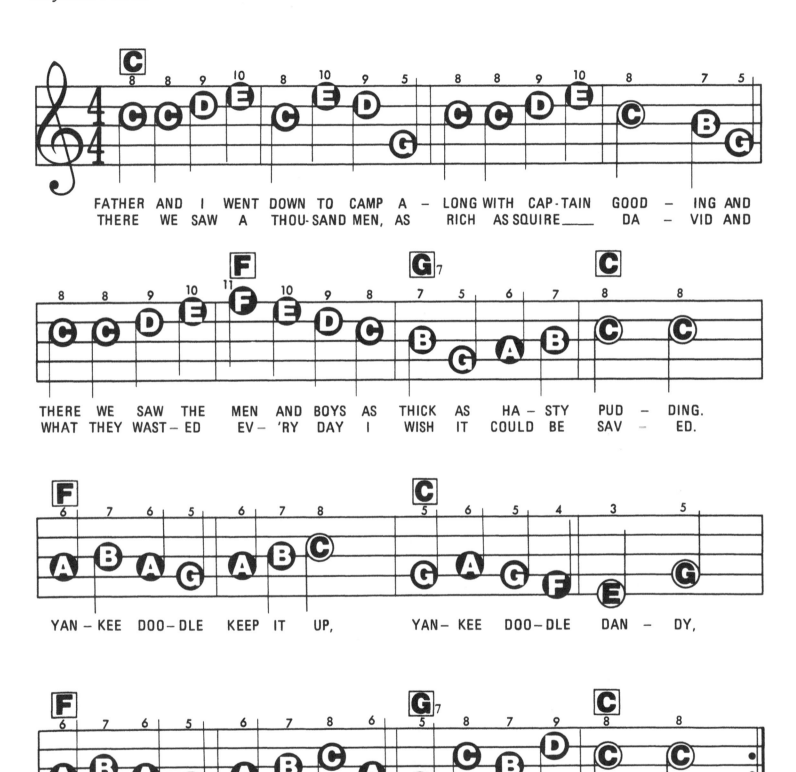

WHISPERING HOPE

Registration 3
Rhythm: Waltz

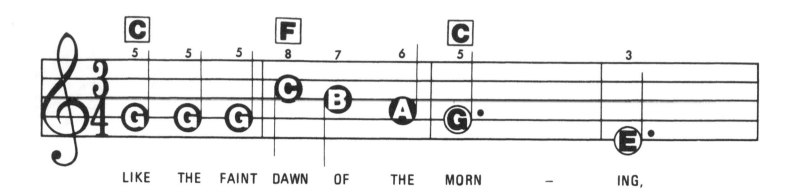

LIKE THE FAINT DAWN OF THE MORN — ING,

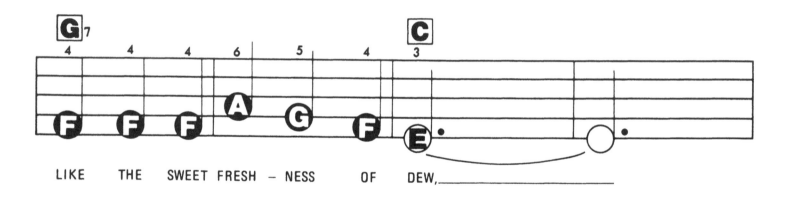

LIKE THE SWEET FRESH – NESS OF DEW,_____

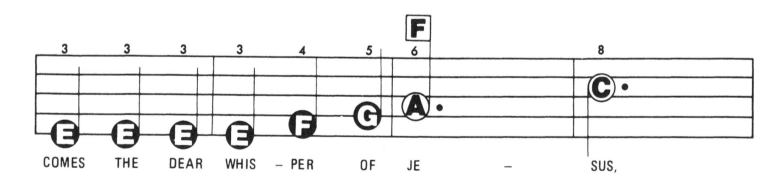

COMES THE DEAR WHIS – PER OF JE — SUS,

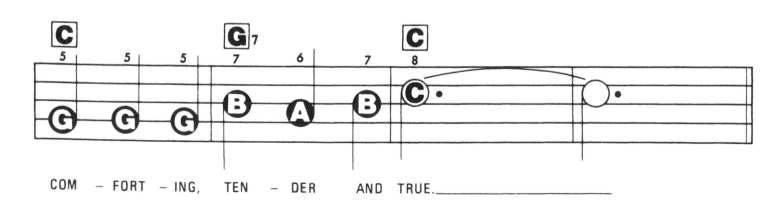

COM – FORT – ING, TEN – DER AND TRUE._____

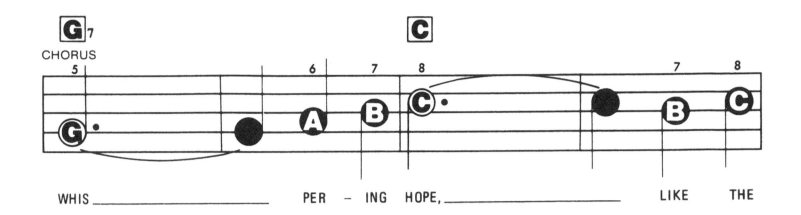

CHORUS

WHIS _____ PER - ING HOPE, _____ LIKE THE

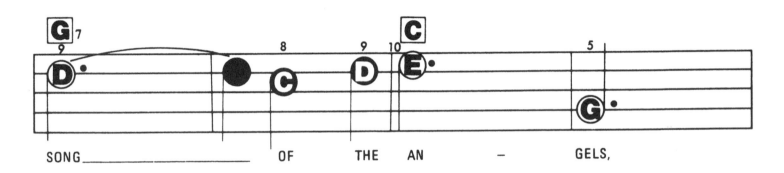

SONG _____ OF THE AN - GELS,

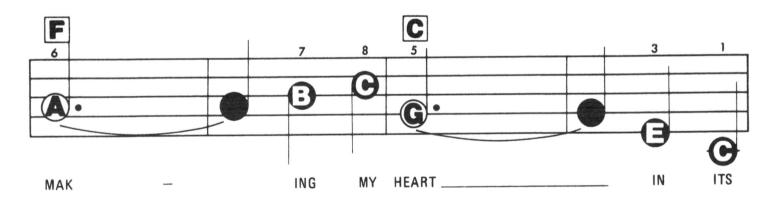

MAK - ING MY HEART _____ IN ITS

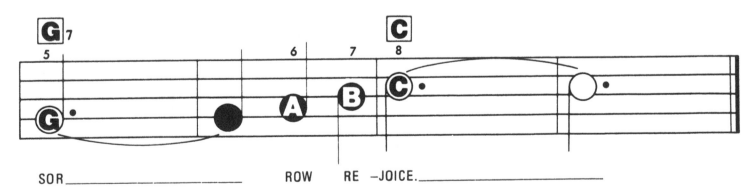

SOR _____ ROW RE - JOICE. _____

2. SINGING THE SONG OF FORGIVENESS,
   SOFTLY I HEAR IN MY SOUL,
   JESUS HAS CONQUERED FOREVER
   SIN WITH ITS FEARFUL CONTROL

   CHORUS

3. HOPE IS AN ANCHOR TO KEEP US,
   HOLDING BOTH STEADFAST AND SURE:
   HOPE BRINGS A WONDERFUL CLEANSING,
   THRO' HIS BLOOD, MAKING US PURE.

   CHORUS

YELLOW ROSE OF TEXAS

Registration 8
Rhythm: March or Fox Trot

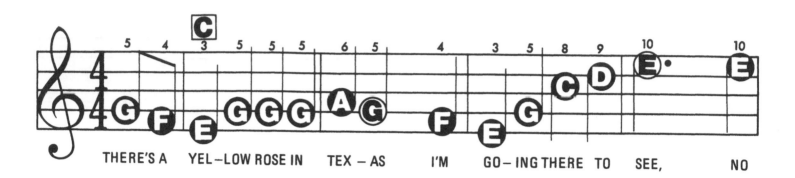

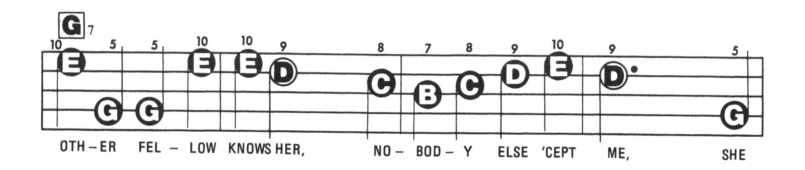

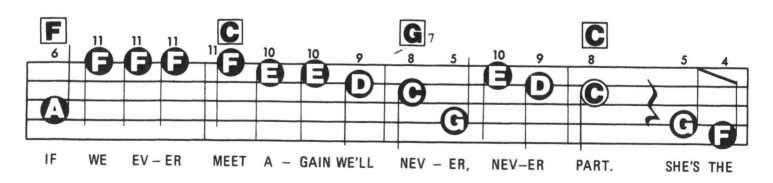

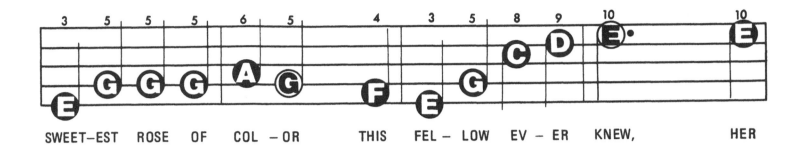

SWEET—EST ROSE OF COL—OR THIS FEL—LOW EV—ER KNEW, HER

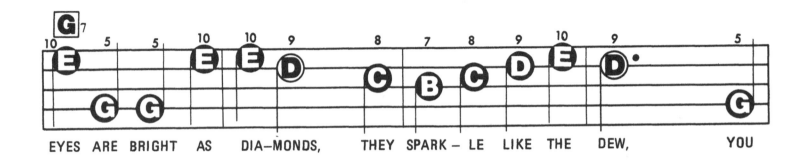

EYES ARE BRIGHT AS DIA—MONDS, THEY SPARK—LE LIKE THE DEW, YOU

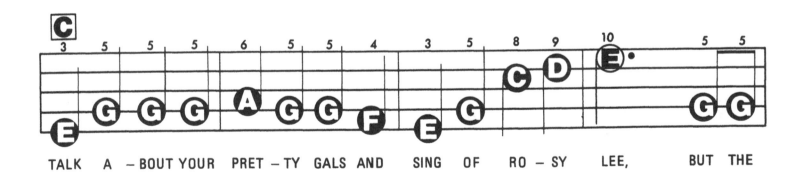

TALK A—BOUT YOUR PRET—TY GALS AND SING OF RO—SY LEE, BUT THE

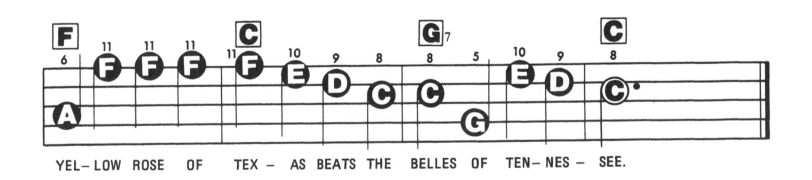

YEL—LOW ROSE OF TEX—AS BEATS THE BELLES OF TEN—NES—SEE.

Registration Guide

- Match the Registration number on the song to the corresponding numbered category below. Select and activate an instrumental sound available on your instrument.

- Choose an automatic rhythm appropriate to the mood and style of the song. (Consult your Owner's Guide for proper operation of automatic rhythm features.)

- Adjust the tempo and volume controls to comfortable settings.

Registration

1	Flute, Pan Flute, Jazz Flute
2	Clarinet, Organ
3	Violin, Strings
4	Brass, Trumpet, Bass
5	Synth Ensemble, Accordion, Brass
6	Pipe Organ, Harpsichord
7	Jazz Organ, Vibraphone, Vibes, Electric Piano, Jazz Guitar
8	Piano, Electric Piano
9	Trumpet, Trombone, Clarinet, Saxophone, Oboe
10	Violin, Cello, Strings